FALAFELS, SOME FROGS AND A FERRET

Simone Mansell Broome

Published by

Llyfrau Cambria Books, Wales, United Kingdom.

Cambria Books is an imprint of

Cambria Publishing Ltd.

Discover our other books at: www.cambriabooks.co.uk

DEDICATION

To the significant women - in memory of my mother, my mother-in-law and all the aunts, and in appreciation of those still carrying the torch - my daughter, granddaughters, daughter-in-law, sister and niece.

Cover art by Cerys Susannah Rees

OTHER BOOKS

by Simone Mansell Broome

Poetry

Not exactly getting anywhere but…(2008)

Juice of the lemon (2009)

Cardiff Bay lunch (2010)

Getting off lightly (ebook - 2021)

A cwtch in Kyrenia - March 2023

Children's fiction

Valletta and the year of changes (2021)

Journal/memoir

Pause - 12 months of going nowhere (2022)

CONTENTS

Fallen

We lived opposite a fallen woman. We knew that's what she was because she was living in sin. And with a married man…which was worse. She was also young, pretty and friendly, and my mum liked her.

The FW and her man – I didn't know what to call him but he wasn't, of course, *her husband* – had two children, twins, a boy and a girl – and an indoor double swing in their attic playroom. I loved swinging on it. I don't remember the names of the children now but I know they shared an initial – maybe they were Roddie and Rosie, or Bernie and Barbara. Something like that.

I've always associated siblings who share the same first letter of their Christian names, (and people whose first name and surname begins with the same letter), with the exotic, the alien and the glamorous. Like Marilyn Monroe, Brigitte Bardot and stars of old movies loved by my father – Claudette Colbert, Simone Signoret, etc. You'll notice the French bias. There were exceptions, like a woman I was friendly with in my early days of motherhood – not alien at all, a sympathetic fellow first timer, but actually rather elegant. And Marilyn and Mervyn, twins, again, who were neither alien nor exotic. I played with them for a short while after we left Wales.

It was a forced friendship. My mother had obviously met their mother somewhere – an achievement in itself as Mum was always working – and arrangements were made. We didn't call them playdates then. I remember ludo, snakes and ladders, a little lukewarm ping-pong and a summer of pretend, dressing-up weddings in our scruffy back garden. Marilyn was a stolid, rather unimaginative child. Mervyn was put-upon but uncomplaining. Wilbur, our first family cat,

1

was usually lavishly costumed and found a small role in the nuptials. The twins and I drifted apart by the time I was eight. There was an older brother who made the skin crawl on the back of my neck. Of course, I never mentioned his creepiness to anyone.

*

The conversations of others have always been fair game. My children used to accuse me of having elephant ears. Much of what I gleaned about fallen women, and indeed the dynamics between man and woman, came from overheard snippets of female chats, confidences, gossip.

You might become a fallen woman, if you let yourself fall for someone, (possibly unsuitable), or fall in love, fall off your pedestal or fall from grace. You could get caught out or caught. You could fall pregnant. And it was a truly terrible thing if this was – *out of wedlock*. A woman's life, it seemed, was about avoiding men while playing some sort of tag, ducking and diving, and running faster. You had to be watchful and wary. And faster. But not in the wrong way. It also, strangely, seemed to be down to women, the ones who *would* get married, to find a man in the first place. And what became apparent to me was that men didn't want to get found or caught. Except the wrong sort.

*

I think my mum was always close to her sister. There were just the two of them. My aunt was creative, practical, talented at all crafts, domestic, a homemaker. She wanted children. She would have loved a daughter. She married, in her early thirties, a divorced man who was bringing up three teenage boys. My aunt then gave birth to two sons. She was one of the very few women I knew, in my childhood, who had encountered divorce in any way at all.

When Mum married and moved to Wales, she lost her sibling and lifelong ally. Mum wasn't really happy in Tenby. I'm not sure what she expected, but I think she must have felt an outsider in a close community. The man she married had four siblings, and, apart from the older sister who had introduced my parents in the first place,

Mum struggled to feel accepted by his family. She worked and she ran a small guesthouse. She was married for five years before having a baby. These things cemented her nonconformity.

She believed herself to be of non-conformist, Protestant stock, with teetotal, puritanical working-class values. In the mix was the Church Army, conscientious objectors and a generation of missing young men – I'm told my grandmother's heart never fully mended. My mother's actual, more mixed, more complex origins we are only now beginning to unravel.

*

In Tenby, it was the other non-locals she became friends with, the Irish and the Italians, hardworking incomers like herself. The people she got to know were all Catholic, and so it was decided that I, and then my sister after me, would attend convents. In my case three of them, until I was eleven; in my sister's, three of them, until she was sixteen. For a while, from when I was eight or nine, I made a rather pretty altar in and around the Victorian fireplace of my bedroom. I had designs on beatification, and, ultimately, canonization, and knew this was a big ask.

My father's older sister, that onetime matchmaker, could have been defined by many as a *fallen woman*. No one would have dared to voice this within earshot of her immediate family. She was long gone from Wales, whilst still in her teens. At several times in her full, colourful life she was a practising Catholic; she numbered priests and monks amongst her acquaintance. This aunt had an eclectic and pragmatic relationship with God in his many earthly manifestations.

The rest of Dad's family was mostly, in a casual kind of way, Church of England in Wales. Lowish. Minimal popery. But not Chapel.

*

At my final convent, nuns filled our heads with the lives of the saints. We were read these stories on rainy afternoons while we worked on bits of handicrafts. Mine were grubby, unpicked, reworked and never finished. My reading matter at the time was a heady combination of

3

illicit ghost stories, tales of the Greek, Roman and Norse gods (and their frankly startling private lives), Shakespeare and children's poetry. The gruesome life and death stories of saints slotted perfectly into this mix. There was torture, execution, martyrdom – the most comprehensive range of savagery.

Female saints seemed to have less exciting lives and far fewer adventures, and they were never really in need of much improvement, of the repentance and reformation type. But they were besieged by men constantly trying to corrupt them spiritually and corporeally. The punishments meted out to female saints were just as horrible as those experienced by the men. And, bafflingly to me at the age of nine or so, the Fall of Man was Eve's fault too. Woman as temptress, aided and abetted by some convenient serpent. I'm as fuzzy now as I was then on the specifics, but the expression I was not to hear for many more years – *it takes two to tango* – did not seem to apply at all to the bible or to ecclesiastical attitudes. Women were bad, *per se*.

I've never had a fondness for incense and always lacked the attention span to sit still throughout the mass…but sin, confession, penance and redemption remain a compelling foursome.

And the flat feet, the slight dyspraxia, (never identified until decades later naturally), and the hole in my heart, didn't predispose me to be good at running fast. Or running at all really. If anything, ducking and diving have been far more my style.

Flitters

There was a new shopping parade in the Berkshire village we moved to from Wales. There was still a village centre about a mile away with an old church, a Victorian school, some cottages and access to a stream which fed into the river Loddon. And then there was the decommissioned aerodrome and the businesses it now housed. The original centre was being usurped, becoming irrelevant by the time we arrived. New housing estates were springing up on all sides. A teacher training college was built, populated and extended. In the ten or eleven years we lived there, the village grew and changed beyond recognition. *Village* no longer seemed to be the right word to define it.

There were flats above the new shops. Two little girls and their parents moved into one of them. They joined my second school, an execrable convent in its final death throes. They wore their uniforms, (grey and maroon), with a certain panache, non-specified hair ribbons and shoes which differed very slightly from the Clarks' specified styles. Outside school, when I went to tea at their flat, their toys were extravagant, cartoon and film-character-inspired. Sweets weren't rationed. Their clothes were new and unusually stylish. Nothing old, shabby, home-made or less than perfect seemed to be allowed to exist in their home. I was quite envious for a while…but they had no garden, were not allowed pets and their mother seemed curiously vacant. She was much younger than our mum.

One early spring afternoon, March probably, in their second term, Mum collected me from school and parked my sister's pushchair at the bottom of the metal steps at the back of the shops. Mum and I climbed the external staircase to ring their doorbell, my sister already protesting loudly from her pushchair. We had decided to have a dressing up tea party in the first few days of the Easter holidays. We were there to deliver an invitation I'd made and coloured in. There was no reply. I told Mum both girls had been away from school that day. We rang again and then, on impulse, Mum climbed up on something – it might have been a milk crate - and peered in a window.

'They're not here,' she said. 'Never mind. Let's go home past the swings.'

I was taken aback by Mum's lack of surprise. The family had gone and we never saw or heard of them again. Of course, I heard the grown-ups talk. Murmurs of debts and gambling. I don't know if it was idle speculation. I don't know what happened to the family next. I only do know that they were the first in a series of 'flitters' I've encountered.

*

There are some flitters too close to talk about, casual or deliberate bounders who've deeply hurt immediate family and good friends. I was mostly too young to know or understand the breadth and depth of it, just that they caused pain and upset, more worry and less money, to people I loved, while they, the instigators of whatever the current chaos was, appeared to move on to start afresh, unencumbered, somewhere else. I remember a couple of late-night visitors trying to collect money owed them by the young family member who'd left precipitately. I remember being rushed upstairs and told to keep quiet until the uninvited visitors had gone.

But these vague recollections were just that. Vague. Impressions. No facts.

*

As a young married woman, I moved to Bristol from London, and then from Bristol to Berkshire, reluctantly, just over seven years later. In Wokingham, three more flitters crossed our paths. The first was, for a short time, our next-door neighbour, a young man oozing ambition and success. Alexander, (this wasn't his real name), was small, dark-haired, wiry and snappily dressed with a big company car.

6

He was something in sales or computers. We rarely spoke – such busy lives – with little in common except physical proximity from time to time.

At weekends, a succession of attractive young women came to stay. There was one who visited a number of times – maybe six or seven – a potential keeper? She always waved, smiled and exchanged greetings. She was pretty, in an estuary ladette kind of way, with long orange limbs and long bright yellow hair. Privately, and quite fondly, we referred to her as 'the bimbo.' Unfortunately, our youngest child, who was then about four or five, heard us. On one visit she rushed out of the front door smiling and shrieking – 'Hello Bimbo. Bimbo, hello, hello.' The girl smiled and waved back but her response was possibly a little cooler the next time...

And then one day I returned from the school run and our neighbour's front door was swinging on its hinges. Wide open. I deposited children and bags and went to investigate. The house was empty. Everything except the fixtures and fittings had gone. There were just a few flyers and unopened letters – the official-looking sort – blowing around in the hall. Apparently, a Dutch removal lorry had arrived earlier. There was no forwarding address. For a few months people knocked on our door assuming we'd know where he'd gone. I seem to remember there was a problem when we tried to buy a new TV on hire purchase, as we shared a postcode with our flitter.

∗

About three years later, my sister married and moved to a large modern house about half a mile away from us, on the same housing estate. Hers was a close of detached houses where each had a view of at least two others from several windows. The flit executed by her neighbours was extraordinary. It was planned audaciously. They were a loud and noticeable family of six, who moved into the double garage of their house, because 'improvements' were ostensibly being made, including the fitting of a new kitchen. So they stripped out the existing kitchen and sold it. And then proceeded to detach, demount and take apart all fixtures and fittings, including carpets, the bath, taps, etc. They were not observed or heard doing any of this.

7

No one expressed any curiosity beyond initial enquiries about the kitchen and the reason for their temporary occupation of the garage. Their exit was even more remarkable in that *no one saw them leave*. Everything that could be unscrewed from wall, floor or ceiling, even the light fittings, was. The interior was denuded, wrenched apart. Again, there was no forwarding address.

*

It was an aspirational, upwardly mobile time and place of much commuting, long hours, huge mortgages and easy credit, of personal status being enhanced by the number of store, loyalty and credit cards you could squeeze into your purse or wallet. We were living in the middle of it and were part of it. Of course, there was soon a financial crash and much social unrest.

The other flitter we encountered back then was a deeply disturbing one. One of his daughters was at nursery with my daughter, the same age as her, but treated like a baby. The other daughter was the same age as my younger son. There were playdates. The family lived in a house halfway between ours and the school and nursery site, so dropping in was convenient. He was an estate agent in the town and she was a 'stay-at-home' mum, devoted to her children and home and on the periphery of the Tupperware set. I liked her. She was gentle and easy to talk to. He was bluff and brash, flashing large rolls of notes. He made me feel uncomfortable.

When they disappeared, I discovered that they'd left money owing to the nursery, that they'd not told school, that no one knew where they'd gone and that it wasn't just me who felt concerned for those two, pale, infantilised little girls. And I discovered that there'd been a birthday party, just before they went, where this man had tried to behave 'inappropriately' with several of the child guests, including my daughter. There was no drama, no outcry, just a collective shudder of recognition. And a sense of relief that he'd gone.

Fur and feathers

All fur coat and no knickers. I inherited my parents' distaste for flashiness. I vividly recall their slightly suspect mistrust of 'new money'. Frankly, any money at all would have been welcome for most of my childhood.

I don't remember Mum ever wearing a fur coat, but several of my aunts owned at least one. It was quite normal then. When very young, maybe aged two or three, I had a velvet bonnet style hat, a fitted velvet coat with a fur collar and a fur muff on corded velvet. It was a deep royal blue. I assume the fur elements were made of synthetic fur but can't be sure. Whatever it was, it was gloriously tactile and I loved it – the whole outfit.

By the time I was in my teens, it was impossible to wear fur and be ignorant of its origins. My aunt, (Mum's sister), gave me a cast-off fur coat, old, rather moth-eaten, dark brown. I wore it guiltily and occasionally, mostly when I saw my aunt. My feeble justification was that the creatures who had given their lives, so that this coat could be made, were long gone. I was reusing, recycling – and making my aunt happy.

There was another coat passed on to me by another aunt, (my father's elder sister), when I was eighteen or nineteen. By then, this aunt was an administrator for a very genteel, old-fashioned charity in London. This second coat was an impractical 1920s cream tapestry affair with a sheepskin collar, cuffs and hem. It probably had once looked stylish on its original human owner, as I'm sure she'd have had cropped hair and a neat little cloche hat, and would have been slender, elegant and a good seven or eight inches taller than me. The effect must have been very different with me wearing it. When my concrete campus was lashed by sideways rain this flapper coat soaked up water, became unbearably heavy and smelt ovine.

These gifts from aunts were well meant. However, nothing would ever have persuaded me to wear an animal around my throat and shoulders and I have always felt total repulsion for such things.

*

I was aware that my parents – their views and attitudes – were not like other parents I came across. They were considered a little eccentric. They were older than my friends' parents, especially in the case of my father. He was thirty-six, *a middle-aged thirty six*, when I was born.

When I was a baby, it wasn't uncommon for occupied prams to be left untended outside houses. Babies or toddlers would nap, cry, gurgle, etc., left to their own limited devices, while mother or carer *got on with things*. On fine mornings, or any mornings when it wasn't actually pouring, I was parked on the narrow pavement outside our house in Tenby. There was an enclosed courtyard at the back of the house so, my theories are - that either the front of the house was sunnier, or that having strangers peering into my pram and cooing at me on a regular basis was considered to be providing me with suitable entertainment. My mother must have assumed that most people like babies and that most people are kind.

This assumption of kindness had not been fully explained to the seagulls. I was once badly pecked whilst in my pram. Maybe I'd just been fed. Something about me in my pram must have appealed to them. I don't know who rescued me, or how long the attack went on for, but it left me with a huge phobia. Of birds and feathers.

When you're a child and you have a phobia, what do you do? Mostly, you don't talk about it. You don't expose your weakness to the world because you do not know for certain that people will be understanding. Generally, you get away with it. No one knows.

*

Sister Rosalie took us girls for weekly nature walks from half term in the Spring term to half term in the Autumn term. This was an easy circular stroll close to the school. We took back wildflowers, ferns, nuts, acorns and leaves. We had a nature table in the corner of our classroom where we displayed and labelled our finds, always being told just to take one or two examples, never to be greedy. On the wall behind our table, we pinned rubbings of bark and leaves, pictures of the cloud formations on the afternoons of our walks, drawings of butterflies, moths and ladybirds. Sometimes there was a small dead insect. Sometimes there was a broken bird's egg. Occasionally, and terrifyingly, there was a bird's nest or a feather. And I would do my very best to make sure I didn't touch it, and that my fear wasn't spotted.

Someone did notice. There was a particularly nasty child who tormented me for three years, dead birds in my desk or my satchel – that kind of thing. She was physically cruel too and my knee is still scarred from a deliberate act of malice, one of many. We went our separate ways at eleven. I met her again at a party when I was twenty one. She made a joke about childhood squabbles, and I knew absolutely that *I did not and could not forgive her. I never saw her again.*

Another horrible memory is of going to play for the day at a house I'd never visited before and discovering that the amusement planned before lunch was a bicycle ride, through the extremely free-range chicken farm next door. I've always lacked both balance and co-ordination; bikes and me have never made easy companions. But a chicken farm as well! I survived, but it was the stuff of many nightmares.

One of the odder ideas my parents toyed with was – buying a chicken farm on the Isle of Wight. We had already spent two or three holidays there and my parents seemed to like it. Our first dog, Rowlie, was bought from the island, from a fabulously raffish home, occupied by a chain-smoking woman who had henna-dyed curly hair and wore some kind of silk kimono, and her uniformed and much younger chauffeur. Rowlie, his boisterous siblings and his weary, good-natured mother seemed oddly out of place in that household.

11

In my parents' briefly considered poultry farm scheme, my phobia did not figure as an impediment.

*

Wilbur, my first pet, a neutered tabby male, was a killing and maiming machine. While I always felt sad when he delivered a kill to us, even if it was a bird, it was far, far worse when he brought home something feathery and *wounded*. My father would want to leave well alone, let nature take its course; my mother would want to nurse it back to health, feed it water by syringe, keep it in a shoe box punctured with air holes, find it worms, etc.

I would want to be as far away as possible from Mum and her latest hopeless cause.

Now, the phobia has become a kind of allergy as well. If I'm unlucky to sleep a night in a room with any kind of feather bedding, pillows, etc., I wake with a blocked nose, streaming eyes, a tight chest, so it's almost the first thing I ask about when planning to stay anywhere.

People are sometimes disbelieving, or disparaging – why haven't you had therapy, dealt with it, that kind of thing? I have tried many different strategies over the years. Nothing has worked in that my phobia is still very much alive and well. I don't feel damaged or diminished by it. My phobia is just part of my past and who I am now. Part of me.

Frozen

It didn't matter that our TV was black and white. There were no colours. This was the winter of the snow, the snow which lasted until Easter. Months of whiteness. Before, if we'd had any snow, it was just a few inches for a few days. At worst, a foot or so for a week. Rarely any deeper or longer.

We always wanted it to come at Christmas, part of the package deal with sleighs and reindeer, but this wish was almost never granted. That year, the TV reminded us to feed the wild birds and make sure our pets were in and safe at night. There was endless footage of farmers battling through white lanes with high snowdrift hedges, trying to get fodder to those animals who were unlucky enough to winter outside. Those they were able to find. Animals froze to death. Water became thick, impenetrable ice. Birds and fish starved.

It was a quiet time, not a time of frivolity. After the novelty of the first few pristine days we didn't play outside any more. With no central heating and the insides of windows jewelled with intricate ice patterns, getting your clothes wet was discouraged. The snow seemed to soak up everything, to deaden all sound. It was a time of solidarity, of neighbourliness, of focussing on the basics.

Where we were, in the South, in Berkshire, buses continued to run, schools stayed open and were warmer than our homes. In our classroom, and in the hall, hats and gloves, scarves and socks steamed dryish on the old cast iron radiators all day. The nuns took our small frozen bottles of milk, (delivered before daylight), out of the crates they had arrived in and lined them up on the floor of the hall so that each one was touching some small part of pipe or radiator. Our days were shifted around. There was no outside play, and nothing like P.E., country dancing or choir was allowed to happen until after break, when all hazardous glass was out of the way.

And if we complained about our lives being confined, there were always the examples of other parts of the country, where the snow was thicker, where roads were impassable, where normal life was suspended. Life in those places was about survival, about coping. Not about being a bit more difficult or restrictive or inconvenient.

In early February, Wilbur disappeared. My sister and I were desperately upset about this. The longer he was gone, the less likely it was that he'd still be alive. Our parents didn't spell this out to us, but we had access to regular gloomy sources of news which underlined his probable fate to us.

When the snow finally melted, our world was revealed again, the shape of gardens and hedges, the definition between pavements and roads, the outline of branch and twig on the trees which hadn't collapsed under the weight of it all. There was colour too, even if most of it was a limited, drab kind of palette. Our front garden was hidden from the road by tall laurel hedges on both sides of the wooden gate. When the hedges became visible once more, we found Wilbur under one of them, frozen, so close to home. This was, of course, terribly sad for us children.

Our family's loss was shared by at least seven other cat-loving families in the village. All eight cats had been poisoned by a crazy person. He had used the blanket of snow as cover for his pet killing, while the rest of us were watching out for neighbours, throwing crumbs and crusts out for the birds and just getting by, getting through it.

*

In Bristol, years later, I remember one year of heavy snow. Not extreme and long-lasting like the childhood year I've just recalled, but a period of maybe two or three weeks when normal life stopped. Cars stayed outside, stationary in their white blankets. Few people went to work or school for a while. Families spent time together. It was almost Dickensian. We still had no central heating but we did have gas fires by then, (three I think), two of our windows were double-glazed, and the rest had been refurbished so they didn't rattle any more. There was also a tumble dryer – new, hard-working and much appreciated - which I used for drying nappies.

I was extremely pregnant with baby number three and seemed to spend my days hauling the two little boys around, as well as whatever shopping I was able to buy, on a homemade wooden sled. In deep snow, the double buggy was redundant. The toddlers loved the sled. I did not go into premature labour. I must have been much fitter then.

*

When we moved home from Bristol to Berkshire, two houses later, it was February, just before half-term. It was bitterly cold, rain turning to sleet turning to snow as we travelled East. The move was incident-free until we neared Wokingham.

The house we were moving into was a mid-terrace, and access for all our worldly goods was in through the back gate and down the path. There was nine inches of snow in this back garden. A miniature hedge was obscured by the snow. The two removal men, (who were probably not best pleased with the change of weather anyway), tripped over this low obstacle while carrying a sofa. One of them fell and hurt his back. He spent the rest of the day in the cab of his lorry. Desperate times call for unorthodox measures. It was my husband who drafted himself in to help. I was of little practical assistance as I was encumbered with three small children and a cat. It was also barely nine weeks since I'd been in hospital with meningitis.

The day did finally come to an end, with all our possessions dragged off the lorry and into the shoebox which was to be home for the next two years. All floors were filthy with the snow we'd tramped in. The removal men left, much later than they, and we, had anticipated. I've moved many times. This move is etched in memory as one of the most disorganised, most exhausting and most painful.

When we'd finally made up beds and dispatched the children upstairs, the husband informed me that the man who'd injured himself had recently had back surgery. This news had been passed on

15

by my weary spouse's temporary workmate. The man who fell was on his first job after returning from sick leave. I had nursed unsympathetic, unpleasant and frankly evil thoughts towards him all day. He had abandoned us, *the lightweight, the malingerer*, preferring to lurk in his cab while we struggled on without him.

After that, I felt guilty for a few moments, and then allowed myself *just a little* grudging sympathy with my bedtime cuppa.

Fair

Picture this small child, a girl. She has blonde curls, though not as exuberantly, abundantly cherubic as those which two of her children will be blessed with. Her head and bottom are round, arms still toddler-plump, legs likewise, shoulders narrow. She is standing on something – a bed, a chair, a chest? You can't see but somehow she has climbed up onto whatever it is and is now up on tiptoe, straining to see out of her attic window.

It's the music which has called her, the unmistakeable tinny clarion call. The fair has come to town. She fancies she can see the swing-boats as they reach the top of their arc, plunge down and then are visible for a brief moment again. She longs for those swing-boats, for someone to take her to the fair.

I was still an only child, not yet at my first school, not yet attending nursery, my only regular contact with other children being with the twins who lived across the street from us. I spent most of my time with adults, or on my own, amusing myself. The yard at the back of our house in Tenby backed onto the churchyard. I don't reckon the church authorities would have permitted a fairground to be set up amongst the graves, so somehow this *memory* must be part truth, part dream or several recollections spliced together.

*

In our *village* in Berkshire, we lived opposite a park, established around, and named in honour of, the Coronation. The swings, slide and other play equipment were at the far left corner of a huge swathe of green. The fairground used to set up on that field for about a week– I don't think it was every summer – but several times while we were there. By this time, fairs were not just other-worldly, magical places where the music beckoned and the swing-boats thrilled. They were associated with other things too. Gaudy, chipped paintwork, oily engine smells, carousels where the horses had unbelievably sad eyes, hordes of grubby men with loud voices and their shirtsleeves rolled up. And danger. As we grew older we were allowed to cross the road and play in the park unaccompanied. Never at fair time.

Some other girls, older girls, were allowed to attend without adults. There were clucks of disapproval, nods and shrugs. I sensed something might happen, probably did happen to *those girls*. We were not permitted to share in whatever it was.

*

I remember a balcony at the back of a house in the Pyrenees. Our hosts invited us to watch with them. The troupe, who had arrived to set up at one end of the long promenade, was called *a travelling circus*. They were part-circus, part-fair and totally entrancing. The music which played was different this time – an alien mix of Europop, mournful Eastern European ballads, folk tunes and much fiddle playing. There were jugglers and fire-eaters, acrobats, an ancient carousel, a fortune-teller in a curtained booth, stalls where you could win a coconut or a startled looking teddy, a desperately sad pair of harlequins, and a sparkly woman who rode bareback on two white ponies, doing handstands and leaping from one pony to the other. There were a couple of food stalls and, best of all, there were swing-boats.

The first evening, we just watched excitedly from above. The second evening our parents relented and we were taken to share in the magic. There was a young boy with not many brown teeth, who passed a hat round. He was barely taller than me and I think he had a small monkey on his shoulder, but that could have been a second boy. They all left the next day, giving the promenade back to the sightseers and the old men.

*

I've had my fortune told only once, in Brighton. I was nineteen or twenty. The gypsy read my palm and used her crystal ball as well. I was with a friend and we dared each other to do it. She predicted much love, two marriages, three children. *Sons*. I was sceptical in the extreme. About the sons in particular. I am one of two sisters, as was my mother, and her mother had two sisters. But I have had three children, two sons and a daughter. I have been married once and am still married. Though it is true that I've had to kiss *a fair few frogs*.

*

My father had a highly developed sense of what was just. *Unfairness* riled him in the extreme. I remember him spending hours writing, editing and perfecting long letters of complaint or protest. I remember the pride he took in these letters, and his sloping handwriting. I have no memory of my mother's handwriting, or, indeed, of her writing anything at all.

With the benefit of hindsight, much of my father's indignation and outrage was misguided. Although I realised some of his shortcomings, I adored him and always wanted to please him. The total collapse of my secondary school existence was, in part, due to his concept of *fairness*. He was an intelligent man who'd had, because of poverty, to leave Narberth Grammar School at thirteen. He was required to help support his motherless family. Someone kindly offered to sponsor him to complete his education, but he was unable to accept.

Our education was important, vital even, to him. When he realised that the sciences were not calling me, he set his heart on me studying classics. Ancient Greek was an option at school. I had just started Latin and was ambivalent about it, though the history fascinated me, and I still derive huge pleasure from seeing the Latin roots of words.

Dad urged me to go for Greek. At the end of my third year, we received notice that Greek was no longer going to be offered, and that I would be taking German instead. I don't know why. Maybe I was the only one to choose it.

The letters began to flow. My father felt it was not *fair*, it was not right and I *must* be allowed to learn Greek. The headmistress, whose surname was Hardcastle, was unmoved. I was to start German in September. My father kept writing. Nothing changed. He either suggested, or told me, not to attend German classes until the misunderstanding was resolved.

This was, if not how it began, how it accelerated into disaster. I skipped classes. Detentions multiplied. I skipped school. I had migraines, period problems, fainting fits and then anorexia. My periods stopped; I was put on the pill for a while; I gained weight and some sort of equilibrium, but not for long.

My sixteenth year was blessed with a trinity of insomnia, nightmares and depression. I had almost two academic years of patchy, and then no, school attendance. Shortly after my sixteenth birthday, I was admitted to an adolescent unit in a mental hospital in the Home Counties. I was there for about two and a half months, not as ill, I felt, as some of my fellow patients, but definitely unable to cope.

When I came out of hospital, it was the beginning of the shift in my parental influences. While I still admired my father in many ways, his clay feet were becoming visible. I began to appreciate Mum.

*

Mum's only sister had two sons. One was eleven months younger than me, slightly skinny with straight dark hair and brown eyes. The other was two or three years younger, with blonde curls and startlingly blue eyes. Harvey developed leukaemia shortly after his second birthday. His parents were distraught. The whole family stayed with us often that year. There were appointments, second opinions, transfusions, third opinions, despair and tears. Survival rates from leukaemia were much lower then.

Harvey died days after his third birthday. It was the first death I was aware of. The randomness of his loss was appallingly cruel. Death of a small child, of this small child, of any small child, can *never* be just, *never* be fair.

Fertility

Apparently, sex was discovered in 1963. Though, like the Americas, it might have existed quite happily by itself before then. I knew there were no gooseberry bushes under which babies might be found. In the long back garden of our Victorian red brick semi we had gooseberry bushes in abundance, also white, red and black currant bushes, and almost a small orchard of wizened apple and fruitful Victoria plum trees. No bulrushes. Not a swaddled baby or a stork in sight. The first storks I ever saw were decades later, nesting in chimney pots and on church towers, while I was holidaying in Greece.

A childhood friend had a prolific tabby cat. I saw plenty of newborn litters of helpless, blind kittens, even at the moment of their arrival. Their ultimate fate was appalling, and glossed over by the adults. I knew perfectly well where babies came from. It was how they got there which remained a mystery.

*

At school, boys were allowed to attend until seven, but there were only a handful of them, adored younger brothers of tribes of girls. Pupil names, apart from a few Marys, a Teresa and a Bridget, were dominated by the 'eens' (and 'ines'). We had Noleen, Colleen, Pauline, Eileen, Christine, Maureen, Noreen, Josephine, Doreen, Kathleen and Geraldine – at least one of each, probably more.

Noreen was the youngest of nine and felt it to be her duty to enlighten her peers about the mechanics of conception. But I'm afraid, despite much giggling and whispering, I was to leave junior school not much wiser. Immaculate Conception remained my only, decidedly dodgy, theory.

21

Around my thirteenth birthday, I started my first part-time job, Saturdays and holidays, in the chemist's shop on the parade at the top of our road. I had to wear a scratchy nylon overall, (several sizes too big for me and I vaguely remember stripes). I scraped back my hair into a high ponytail, or into the neatest plaits I could achieve. More of a mouse than a blonde by then. The chemist's was an independent business. I think the people who owned it had either two or three – no more.

It wasn't a huge shop, but, as well as dispensing prescriptions, it sold a vast variety of treasures. There was the baby section with infant formula, baby foods, bibs, rattles, teething aids and sterilising paraphernalia; ladies' essentials like the monthly consumables I was already familiar with; ladies' luxuries like stockings, cosmetics, hair dyes, wash-in, wash-out tints, harpins, hair nets, bath salts, bath cubes, scented soaps and talcum powders. A whole aisle was given over to products for hair, skin and teeth. There was a small gift and toy section of mostly questionable taste, a smaller section of 'diet foods' I would get to know far too soon. And during my two years of working there, an exciting twirly foot care display stand arrived with an even more exciting range of *exercise sandals*. These were not allowed to be worn at work because they required bare legs and feet. In the interests of health and safety, (which I'm not sure had been discovered by then), this was a big no. In the interests of modesty also, as no day passed without climbing a ladder, I remain grateful for this stipulation.

There were also the things you had to ask for, at the counter, lest you injured yourself with them, like aspirins, razor blades or rat poison. And there were the items you whispered your request for, with a hand shielding part of your face. When I started working there, there were always at least three of us working - me, (stocking the shelves, unpacking boxes, climbing up and down ladders, making tea and generally running errands), the dispensing chemist, (who wore a white coat), and one or two older ladies. The first time I was behind the counter, (by now trusted with taking money, wrapping things, etc

), and I was approached by a man who wanted to buy *something he needed to ask for*, the woman working that shift and the pharmacist both rushed to my aid, pushing me out of the way in their enthusiasm to shield my innocence..

*

It was the end of the sixties. Things changed. The contraceptive pill was handed out all and every day and I was soon trusted to do this, despite my childish appearance and remaining vestiges of ignorance. Staffing levels slowly decreased.

Over the months I found out that the chemist had a problem, a quite serious, accelerating drink problem. It was our collective duty to shield him from exposure, and disgrace. This I was told over tea and a dunked custard cream. But I knew it already. He had started going for rests, a little lie-down, a quiet cigarette at the back of the shop. Soon he would sleep for the majority, if not all, of his shift. I was often left to cash up, to turn out lights and the little heater we had at the back in winter. I locked up. Where was he? Did he have a flat above the shop? Did he remove his white coat and stagger off home? I don't remember.

On many occasions I dispensed alone, deciphering medical hieroglyphics, counting out tablets, labelling bottles with 'three times daily after food' and the like. I didn't tell my parents about this, as I quite liked the responsibility and felt, in my bones, that they might possibly disapprove. As far as I'm aware, *no one died*.

Something happened though. Did the business fold? Did someone tell my parents? By the time I was fifteen, I had a new Saturday and holiday job, in the milk bar and café at the front of the Dairy. A few doors away from home.

*

Small morsels of knowledge steadily wiped out my ignorance. Nothing from my parents. Nothing from school until we all knew anyway and were forced to spend an afternoon, a hot sticky afternoon, in the company of a coerced male parent. Conversations overheard and female colleagues collectively enlightened me. Not getting pregnant was the key lesson.

There was a pretty girl living in a caravan in the garden of our neighbour over the road. She had a daughter, aged two or three, who was equally pretty and wore matching clothes. The mother was obviously skilled at dressmaking. She was eighteen or nineteen and deeply disapproved of. My mother pitied her. *She had ruined her life.*

I have conflicting memories of my mother's views on sex. Her language could be quite fruity. She delighted in being outspoken, in shocking people sometimes. She was a nurse for much of my childhood, and had no coyness about either the naming of parts or about wandering around semi-clad. She embraced contraception and wasn't shy about promoting it. But she had an absolute horror of termination. Some of this may have been influenced by the Catholic values she was surrounded by, but some of it dated from her time as a young (too young) pupil nurse in London at the end of the war. She had dealt with the aftermath of desperate women who'd had backstreet abortions which had gone wrong, or worse, who'd tackled their problem with a knitting needle. So traumatised was she by these experiences that I was never ever going to be able to confide in her about sex.

*

It seemed so unfair that she was suddenly gone just as I reached adulthood. I would have loved her to have been my confidante, advisor and companion when I became a mother. She would have loved being a grandmother. Pregnancy loved me and I loved it, positively blooming, thriving, flourishing each time. Birth and the days and weeks following were much less easy for me.

*

I have always loved the shape and sound of words, often reading out loud when I'm alone. To me, it's tactile, palpable, involving all the senses. I have heard some consider *plinth* to be the sexiest word in the English language, a perfect synchronicity of voice box, palate, teeth, tongue and lips. I would assert that *fecund* and *fecundity* come a close second and third place.

24

Falafel

A small round patty popular in Egypt, the Middle East, the Mediterranean. Made of chickpeas, fava beans or both. Unfairly perhaps, because the recipes are not complex, I have coined the verb 'to falafel', intransitive, meaning to waste time by fussing, to over-complicate a process, to enjoy fiddling about, riffing in a desultory kind of way. See also 'to faff' and 'to fanny'. Often followed by 'about'.

Falafels have been around for about two thousand years. They are ubiquitous now, but I first met them at uni. I was taken under the wing of a highly intelligent M.A. student, an Egyptian woman in her mid-twenties. She cooked. She loved cooking. She loved cooking for other people. She was kind, funny and effervescent and, for about a year, I talked to her about my messy existence. I was a very immature nineteen-year-old. She was a good, sympathetic listener.

My new friend was living a Western life, relishing her studies; she had just moved to Brighton from Ireland - Dublin I think. She was emerging from a complex relationship with an Irish guy. She spoke sometimes about how temporary she felt her current life was, how she'd have to toe the line eventually, submit to the will of her family, marry someone of their choosing. I thought she was joking.

I met her again three or so years later. I was about to marry. She was married, with a young baby and working for an Arabic newspaper. Her husband spoke almost no English and did not welcome us. We tried to arrange a few catch-ups after that. There was always a reason why she had to pull out at the last moment. I felt she was crushed, her spirit curbed, her bright future dimmed. I may have misjudged the situation, but it saddened me.

*

My father-in-law and mother-in-law were traditionalists about food. Spices were avoided. Garlic was taboo. I was probably viewed as a bit of a challenge as my tastes were not meat-and-two-veg, far from it. Within a year or so of being involved with their son, I was fully vegetarian. As was their son. But when my in-laws were in their early sixties they started travelling to warmer climes for the winter – from just after New Year to about Eastertime. This was partly so that they'd be able to play golf all year round, partly because damp weather was bad for their arthritis, and partly because they thought that if they didn't have to expend vast amounts on heating in the coldest months, they'd be saving money. I'm not sure they really believed in the saving money justification.

Their first winter watering hole was Cyprus. Life in Cyprus for January, February and March suited them very well – they ate out every night. Wine and aniseed liqueurs and local brandy were consumed. They visited local tavernas and sampled local delicacies. Hummus, falafel, olives, etc were enjoyed plentifully. Back in Devon, my father-in-law refused to admit that his tastes had changed or broadened. But they had.

My father and mother were also traditionalists about food, but less so. Dad's food horizons had stretched in war time. He'd spent five years in Egypt, East Africa and the islands off South Africa – Madagascar and Mauritius. He'd eaten with Arabs, Indians, Italians, French and with native tribesmen. Back home, he reverted to what was normal, safe *and cooked for him*, but he retained his openness to different foods.

He had, as had many of his contemporaries, a very sweet tooth – sweets, chocolate, hot drinks laced liberally with sugar and porridge with condensed milk *and* syrup. I rarely saw him drink, but he had an occasional beer at a wedding and a secret partiality for French dessert wine. Monbazillac is the name I remember. After mum died, he drank whisky and cried at the end of my bed for about six weeks.

I came across garlic for the first time at the age of eleven. We travelled to the Pyrenees in the Summer holidays, staying for a while at the home of the parents of one of the nuns at school. It was a

French order but this young teaching nun was the only one who seemed to be, and sounded, French. My father took a liking to her and practised his French on her. They swapped song lyrics, Piaf, Aznavour, Mireille Mathieu and so on. The house in the Pyrenees was a tall, dark, town house with views of the square and of the mountains beyond. Madame shuffled around the house all day with dusters attached to the bottom of her slippers. The house smelt of furniture polish and something else, something unfamiliar. We were not close to the sea but there were nearby lakes with cordoned off swimming pools at their fringes. The water was only shallow for a few feet. Not being a particularly strong swimmer, I tended to hug the edges, which involved getting up close and personal with many of the locals. They all exuded garlic, an alien perfume to me. This was obviously the mystery aroma in our hosts' home.

*

I was vegetarian in spirit long before I knew of the word's existence. I became fully veggie at twenty-three, giving up the what small amount of fish I ate *last*. I've been plant-based, or flegan, (more or less vegan), for a few years now. But not militant about it…and I've learned the meaning of compromise. *Pick your battles.*

It started because I never liked the taste of meat. Then, for years, I could only stomach it if it was disguised and didn't look too 'meaty'. Sentiment, ethics and the planet then stepped in, but they were preaching to the converted already.

At least one of my schools made lunches a nightmare. My left-handedness (knife and fork in the 'wrong' hands) and squeamishness about the food put in front of me got me into a lot of trouble. Whenever possible, packed lunches were my preferred option, and by the time I was at senior school I made my own meal when I got home from school too. My culinary skills were very limited - lots of eggs and lots of cheese. Cheese on toast, or scrambled eggs on toast or a cheese omelette – these I alternated.

Around about this time, weekday family meals became increasingly fractured. My father worked late, or was out pursuing his 'radio ham' hobby or lecturing at evening classes. My mother worked most

27

evenings – she ate with my younger sister before going out. Something was left for my father on a covered plate, to be warmed up over a pan of boiling water. I, of course, self-catered.

I was still considered to be too young to take care of my sister so a young girl would sit with us until my father came home. At weekends we usually ate together. Always at home, never out. There was the occasional cup of tea and piece of cake when on a shopping trip, ice creams on holidays or as a treat from an ice cream van. My parents were frugal about food, considering even fish and chips to be an unnecessary extravagance. But then they paid convent fees for me until I was eleven, and for my sister, until she was sixteen. Their priorities were different.

*

Neither parent was a keen gardener but they had bought a house with productive fruit trees and bushes, so, for ten years, we reaped the benefits. The berries, apples and plums which weren't turned into jam – *always jam*, never chutney or pickles – we children sold at the front gate, in the shade of the tall hedges and an old laburnum tree. We had a table, two chairs, heavy traditional scales, a tin with change in it and brown paper bags. We were left in charge of trading, time-consuming but potentially lucrative. Of course, we ate much of the fruit ourselves.

*

From when I was about ten or eleven, my mother was on some sort of diet most of the time. She gave up sugar in tea and persuaded us to do so too. My father resisted. There were diets featured in the paper, diets in women's magazines, diets in the publications pitched at schoolgirls. My misguided adult colleague in the Dairy ate only grapes, crispbreads and an inordinate quantity of mousetrap cheese for three weeks before her holiday. Results were disappointing apart from increased, and audible, flatulence.

The concept of dietary self-flagellation seeped, from Catholicism, from my mother and from magazines, into my teenage consciousness. I gave up chocolate for Lent and gorged on Easter eggs when Lent was over. My weight dropped to five and a half stones, yet I still believed my thighs were fat and my cheeks too chubby. I was anorexic for almost a year. Yet I wasn't admitted to hospital, and *that part* of whatever problem I had developed, corrected itself slowly. It was a real thing for me, but not, ultimately, a big deal.

Foreign

Life wasn't multi-cultural or multi-coloured. At my third junior school there was one Asian family and a Swedish girl. At my fourth school I only remember one Asian girl, (a scholarship girl like me), and an Anglo-German. Naturally, there were, of course, the Irish and the Italians we knew too. At some stage in my childhood, I remember a Sikh who had Sunday lunch with us for a while. I'm not sure how he crossed our paths.

My mother, also, had a childless nursing friend who adopted a black baby boy. I babysat for him occasionally, which was always painless as he slept very well. His parents left me copious supplies of chocolate and biscuits – another bonus. But, generally, we only encountered people who looked more or less like us.

*

Family history is a mysterious, hybrid beast. The story goes that we were all having breakfast together when my father looked out of the window and saw – the ambulance, (which my mother had bought for fifty pounds), being delivered. This cannot have been so, because of the height of our hedges. What I imagine is that two vehicles arrived – the ambulance and the car which was needed to take away the driver – and that they knocked at our front door, and one of them would have asked – *'where do you want this, madam?'* – like any normal delivery driver. Someone must have directed them past our semi and its twin and round the corner to the end of the garden and space for parking. Family mythology records no shrieks of alarm emanating from my father, just jovial approbation of my mother's surprise purchase.

It is unlikely that he knew about it in advance. How willing he was

30

to embrace her plan of converting the vehicle into a motorhome for us all I am less sure of. But he did, and it is probably the only project I can remember him finishing. Actually, it was never *quite* completed and there were a couple of spectacularly inconvenient mechanical breakdowns over the years. But it was finished enough to carry us around Europe.

Holidays, for the next seven or eight years, were taken care of. My sister and I must have been excited initially, but the ambulance was smelly and noisy. Extremely. I was approaching the age when I wanted to fit in with my peers, or sometimes I did. This was a further example of how different my family was from those of my contemporaries, a definitive nail in the coffin of conformity (or non-conformity). The ambulance wasn't viewed, I felt, as cool or trendy – just odd. Our holidays in it, I felt, weren't viewed as exciting or different. Just odd. I shouldn't have minded, but I did. With the benefit of hindsight, this seems not just another example of youthful awkwardness, feeling like an outsider in my peer group, but more a reflection of the narrowness of the world I was growing up in.

My classmates went on package holidays to the Channel Islands, or to Spain. Or to holiday camps. Or the posher ones *took* a house, or cottage, in Cornwall or Norfolk for a month or so. Or they stayed with family who lived by the sea or in the proper countryside. No one else had an ambulance.

Dad was fluent in French – we hadn't known before quite how good he was. Some of his slang was over twenty years out of date, but he could communicate perfectly. He denied any expertise in German or Italian but somehow dredged up enough language to more than get by. He acquired more vocabulary and more confidence as we travelled. Mum spoke not one word of anything other than English. She managed the essentials with particularly enthusiastic mime and signs.

Both parents unwound in the sun – the two preceding holidays had been damp affairs of bed, breakfast and evening meal, the four of us staying in one family room - damp and cold in the Trossachs, unseasonably squally and chilly in Shanklin. Both parents had fallen in gluttony with the honey lemon spread made by our Scots landlady, a bit like lemon curd but with an extra hit of mellifluousness – she guarded the recipe like a state secret, but did try to send Mum a jar after we returned home. I say *try*. It arrived as a sticky mess, broken glass, brown paper and string. None was rescuable.

The Isle of Wight lady had a thing about pottery rabbits. Various sized bunny moulds had been fired, of rabbits in exactly the same sitting position. They were in a range of mostly pastel colours and they proliferated all over the little guest house – at the sides of the front steps, in the porch, on the hall table, on every window sill and shelf, up the stairs. They were used as doorstops. They held meetings in the bricked up fireplaces, exchanged confidences behind twitching net curtains.

The weather, that holiday, was dreadful. I spent much of the fortnight counting and naming each and every rabbit, occasionally rearranging them when I felt I could achieve this unobserved. My names for every bunny, in excess of a hundred as I recall, began with the letter 'B'.

In the ambulance we had no landladies to contend with and the sun shone fiercely for most of the time. We took teabags, white sugar (for Dad), tins of butter, tins of marmalade and paper knickers. Mum had heard that foreign butter was unsalted, that marmalade was unobtainable and that tea would taste different, if we could locate it at all. We discovered French bread, local cheeses and honey, markets selling white peaches and grapes and tomatoes which smelt of sunshine. Our budget was always relatively tight. There was almost no eating out and we picnicked every day.

My sister and I hated the paper knickers. They were uncomfortable in design and they scratched our thighs. Quite reasonably, Mum was trying to reduce chores whilst maintaining standards.

*

This was of course before the EU. You were acutely aware of customs and excise, of how much of what commodity could be bought in country A and brought into country B. Borders were real and were manned by soldiers with guns. Moving from one country to another was a significant event. My father worked for the Ministry of Defence, although he always had something else, (part-time lecturing or a money-making scheme destined for failure), *on the go too*. He was contractually obliged to tell his employers where he was travelling to, and, in some cases, to seek permission. There was a perceived risk. Was it to us, his family? Was it to national security? I can't think that he would have been that important a cog in the machine. All I know is that my seemingly shy, reserved, law-abiding mouse of a father contained within him streaks of recklessness and of extreme arrogance.

Our itinerary was often deviated from – for the hell of it. He liked to be spontaneous. He was less than honest with his employers. He also enjoyed, albeit on a somewhat small scale, breaking the rules. Smuggling. Watches, jewellery, tobacco, cigarettes, brandy, wine. It must have been done for other people – we were a non-smoking, infrequently drinking household. We had little spare cash for jewellery and watches, although Mum had a good eye for quality and craftsmanship. Someone must have advanced us the money. It's a bit of a mystery, but I'm sure Dad's lawbreaking wasn't for profit. The ambulance was always much heavier on the return crossing.

We had one very close shave with uniformed, armed men. There was a flat tyre as we crossed a border. The ambulance was packed with I suppose what could be defined as *contraband*. Even Mum's bra was loaded with extra cargo. She was so angry with my father that time, not her usual eruption of rage which would burn out in minutes. This was different: she seethed and sulked silently for weeks. *He* curbed his more irregular activities after that.

*

Foreign, until I left school, always meant by *our ambulance* or by car, and by ferry. We didn't fly and there was no tunnel. I went on one visit to Paris with a girl from my school the Easter before 'A' levels, when we travelled by coach, ferry and train.

Little remains of that trip except fleeting memories of being hungry all the time, being appalled when we were told one evening

33

that the meat on our plates, (which I was toying with anyway), was horse and not beef, a severely suited Madame who spoke in gruff tones about café life and Jean-Paul Sartre while chain-smoking in class, and running the daily gauntlet of being leered at and fondled on the Metro.

I also had a brief crush on one of the boys from another school. We were gauche, bookish, anxious teenagers. It was never going anywhere. The return ferry crossing was rough. I was violently sick for two days afterwards.

Flooding

It was January 1ˢᵗ and I could have killed for tea. I had no idea what the time was but we hadn't returned home till about 1.30. It was perhaps nine? Or ten? We had been celebrating the season at one of the village hostelries – a Western themed murder mystery night. After a moment of initial diffidence, I had embraced my allocated saloon floozie part, switched the override button, flirted for the county and imbibed much.

The dog was snoring. The cats were absent. The husband was prone in our shipwrecked bed, his mouth slightly open. There seemed absolutely no chance of him making breakfast or even just a brew. Resigned and barefoot, I padded down the steep cottage stairs, my head throbbing gently, my dressing gown loosely wrapped. As I stepped off the bottom stair, I put my foot and dressing gown hem into two or three inches of water. My brain was not yet functioning properly. It took a few seconds to realise that our home was flooded.

What should have been a lazy day, recovering quietly, sending New Year messages, thinking about - *but not* - hoovering up pine needles, and eating festive leftovers, became instead a day of frenzied activity. A day of lifting, stacking, rescuing, mopping and wiping, and of pulling up the old carpet which had covered most of downstairs. It was a grim, damp, brown, smelly kind of New Year's Day.

We were living, though we barely realised it, as the river was a long way off, on the Loddon flood plain. Normally, there wouldn't have been a problem but the council that year, in an outpouring of ecological awareness, had decided not to clear the deep ditches bordering most of the village lanes. So as not to disturb the water voles. We were there for barely four years. It happened once to us.

35

Maybe the council joined up the dots after that.

*

Two houses before, I used to walk the children to and from school, about a mile each way, from our estate across the open land which led to the school and nursery. There was water meadow, light deciduous woodland and a stream. For us, spotting a vole was an occasional, and magical, highlight.

*

Before photos were digital, we possessed packets and packets of pictures from holidays, days out, birthdays and special occasions. Some we took to Boots to be developed and printed; some we sent away. I lost most of them when our cellar flooded in the late 90s.

We were living then in a lovely early nineteenth century house – lovely but in the wrong location. It was on a busy road, which was growing ever busier. It was very close to a roundabout. When lorries passed, the windows rattled and the house shook. If we could have picked it up and placed it down again in a different location, I could have stayed there forever. The headroom in the cellar was extremely low, maybe just over four feet. All you could use it for was storage. So we did. Boxes of books and boxes of photos. *Upset* doesn't come close to the way their loss affected me. After the watery incident, the cellar was tanked, the headroom reduced further and the space became even less usable.

*

One Easter, on Corfu, we were staying in a little house about a mile and a half from the village shops and tavernas. There were two ways in. Either you walked across fields until you joined the only road, or you followed a stream until you met a bridge which then led you to the beach. It was then half a mile or so of sand before turning up into the village.

There were three days of torrential rain. The stream became a small river, bursting its banks, and the bridge collapsed. News spread. Local men worked together, patching it up as if building a sandcastle, with mud, stones, driftwood and anything else they could gather. The next day the bridge was restored and the sun shone for the remainder of our two weeks. We were told the rains happened almost every year around that time. And that the bridge never lasted more than a twelvemonth.

*

My mother died when I was twenty one. For years, at least twelve, she had experienced *women's problems*, heavy, frequent and painful periods. She was prone, as she called it, to dramatic episodes of *flooding*. She could be eating a meal, in a shop, at a bus stop, anywhere really, and blood would gush from her, down her legs and onto the floor. Her clothes would be marked unmistakeably. Her situation would be visible, obvious and extremely embarrassing. Thinking back now, I am amazed at how well she coped, how hard she worked, how unflappable she was and how positive she remained.

On one occasion she *flooded* in Reverend Mother's office when she was there for a meeting about me. I was ten years old and was having some sort of brief emotional hiccough at school. The nun had cleaned up Mum, washed her legs, made her rest until the bleeding had abated and then phoned for a taxi to take her home. Mum always remembered Reverend Mother's kindness and practicality. They were allies, friends even, after that.

I bumped into Reverend Mother in a post office queue about twenty years later. She was retired from teaching and living a quiet life with the remaining elderly sisters. She recognised me straightaway and asked after my mother. When I told her about my mother's sudden death, the nun was moved.

'*Such an exceptional woman,*' she said.

I inherited some of my mother's difficulties, heavy and painful periods, but not manifested anywhere near so extremely. Mum had waited until she was fifty for a hysterectomy, although my sister tells me she asked for one much earlier. Mum died in hospital before she reached the operating table.

I had a series of D and Cs, (standard solutions at the time, but with only the briefest of positive outcomes for me), and then, in my early forties, I was offered an endometrial resection. This worked brilliantly and I am grateful for it. The surgeon spoke to me afterwards. He told me I have a heart-shaped uterus, *bicornuate,* something I share with about three per cent of my sex. It's probably a partial explanation for much of my gynaecological and obstetric history.

*

Bleeding heavily is a terrifying experience. My first bleed was caused by an infection after a tonsillectomy when I was six. I had been home two days. There was panic amongst the adults. Cold flannels and bags of ice were packed around my neck. An ambulance came and took me back to hospital, where I spent a second week recuperating. When I came home I contracted most of the childhood illnesses – chicken pox, mumps, measles and German measles – in swift succession, resulting in my absence from school for about a term and a half. For six weeks of that time I was in bed.

The second unexpected bleed happened in our flat in Bristol four weeks after my first baby arrived. I'd been managing well, recovering fast from surgery, able to lift and bathe my newborn, coping with the steep external staircase. I didn't know what was happening to me, but the *flooding* wouldn't stop. I called the surgery from our neighbours' phone. I think my husband was called too. The doctor who arrived was newly qualified, only a couple of years older than me. He drove me to hospital and dropped off my baby with the couple in the upstairs flat until Roger could get back from work. I was losing the placenta which had been left inside me in the confusion of the emergency caesarean. It set me back for a few weeks.

*

Here in Wales, water and wind dominate our lives for almost half the year. We are at the foot of a bank, but not at the bottom of the hill. When it rains, the lane becomes a stream, washing mud and shale down it, with unexpected islets and rills evolving as it flows. It can appear as if we should temporarily swap our feet and wheels for fins, canoes and paddles. We anticipate some kind of damage, some kind of disruption but hope it's fleeting and minimal. Less than a quarter of a mile further downhill it does flood. As well as streams and rivers, the village houses are blessed with *underground* waterways which bubble up and overflow, leaving mess, mud and mayhem in their wake.

On the plus side, it's green. It's a cliché, but it is. Every shade of green, and of course, *lush*.

Finishing

When I was thirty-six I won a car. It was a black Golf GTI convertible and I kept it for six weeks. The competition was organised by a dishwasher tablet manufacturer - Finish. There was no slogan required. You just had to guess the numberplate, which started with an H and ended with an F. Apparently, I did.

I'm not a frequent enterer of competitions. I don't do the lottery. I'm rarely lucky in charity raffles. But somehow, I won a car. When the phone call came I thought it was a colleague of the husband playing some kind of prank. We didn't call them 'wind-ups' then. I wasn't amused. It was the end of the day and the kids were exhausting me. When the news sank in, I rang the husband and then a few family members. Reactions varied widely from those who were genuinely pleased for me, for us, to those who barely concealed their hostility or envy. A photographer from the local paper turned up and I was asked to smile *winningly*, lean against the car and wave the keys in the air. *Lucky Simone scores a Golf.* The headline went something like that.

We'd just started our own business, giving up two jobs for an uncertain future, where the only certainties were the facts of the largeish mortgage, and our dependents – three children, one dog, one cat. Selling the car furnished our home office with a PC and printer, (ridiculously expensive then), a dedicated phone line and a new phone with answering machine. What was left bought me a much more modest little French car to replace the moribund and ancient Mini. We were not in any position to keep the Golf, but I loved it. I was happy not to be home, babysitting for a neighbour, when its new owners arrived to pay in cash and take the car away. Though reconciled to the decision, I did not want to be there when the transaction took place.

For years afterwards, even when I had become much more aware, as a consumer, of issues like animal testing, sustainability, etc., I would occasionally buy a box or bottle of Finish. *As a thank you.* It was a totally unexpected piece of good fortune which seemed to bless our collective leap into the unknown of self-employment, of starting our first business.

*

My father was a perennial enthusiast, a man of ideas and of projects. He enjoyed working things out but rarely *finished* anything. If it was a private job for someone, then the results were disappointment for the client, and delay in payment or no payment at all for my father. Often the uncompleted project involved him in an upfront outlay as well, so we were doubly out of pocket.

When it came to DIY it was the same story. Schemes were envisaged and decided upon, a plan was started, upheaval was created and then nothing. Because my father was actually highly skilled at a lot of things, it was anathema for him to pay anyone to do anything for us. Money was tight too. But occasionally, in desperation, my mother would just go ahead without him and *get a man in.* We lived in a state of unfinishedness, a state of flux. It became the norm for us as children but was obviously frustrating for my mother. If she didn't ignore him and employ someone without his agreement, then she would occasionally resort to throwing things. She had a fiery temper, but it was over as soon as it erupted.

I remember overheard conversations when she would defend his *not finishing* things to friends or to her sister – '*but at least he's not a drinker or a gambler or a philanderer*'. Several of her close friends were married to men who fell into at least one of the above categories, and one had a husband who hit her. Mum felt our domestic and financial chaos was a small price to pay.

*

At my fourth school, a girls' grammar, there was kudos in suffering. If you were going out with a boy from one of the usual establishments, you swapped scarf tassels with him. When you broke up, whoever finished with whom, it was incumbent on you to grieve noisily and with an audience, in the cloakroom before morning assembly. The cloakroom reeked of melodrama, of teenage rivalries, of hormones. Romantic, and by implication sexual, experience, *however far you'd gone or not gone,* elevated your status with the masses. There were trashy novels; there were song lyrics; there was modern poetry like the Beat poets and then there was the *fast set.* Who needed our limited choice of available soap opera?

I was a slow starter, and by the time boys were on my radar, my situation at that school had broken down. My early romantic beginnings and endings were unshared and *unapplauded.* I wasn't in the cloakroom anymore, or indeed at school at all.

*

I was bad, a couple of times, at finishing destructive relationships. I clung on blindly, hoping for improvement, hoping for change. Two boyfriends at uni were disastrous for me: the first spiralled down into drugs and then dropped out. It was easier to let him go after that. He'd borrowed from me, stolen from me, lied to me and made me believe it was all my fantasy, my failure. My confidence went into freefall, but I finished with him and moved on.

Around the same time, a boy I'd known earlier in my teens wrote to me, wanting to rekindle things, or for forgiveness, or for some sort of closure. His memory of what had happened differed vastly from mine. I didn't correct him. I felt relieved that we were completely finished. In the years since I'd left his tent on the Isle of Wight, he had fallen from what my mother called *the straight and narrow.* He and a small group of his grammar school friends had been involved in armed robbery. A bodged one. I believe a couple of them served short custodial sentences. It was all over the papers, the kind of story loved by journalists. Mum was distraught. He was a rare example of her not getting the measure of someone. '*But he seemed like such a lovely boy,*' she would say, looking genuinely puzzled. I didn't bother to correct her.

The second bad uni relationship lasted longer than the first. We got together, broke up, got together again, broke up again – the pattern repeated. I knew this boy was wrong for me in every possible way. His attitudes were archaic. He wore a black cape and carried a cane. He was emotionally damaged by his upbringing. He shoplifted for kicks and let me take the rap once. He was charming, possessive and jealous, and my self-esteem was undermined every day I was with him. My friends despaired as I made exactly the same mistakes all over again. When it was finished, I had a lot of ground to make up with my degree. I had fallen behind. The final year was hard.

Feet and fingers

As a toddler, I fell a lot. When my mother took me to the doctor, flat feet was the diagnosis, a shallow instep. My feet rolled in slightly. I was prescribed little wedges to be worn inside my shoes to correct the problem. These I wore until I was about eleven. But I continued to fall. When I was two, the GP in Tenby referred me to a cardiologist in Cardiff – I have no idea why that avenue was chosen. The cardiologist told my parents I had a small hole in my heart, not requiring surgery. Just observation and a certain amount of caution. I was seen regularly until the age of seven or eight. With a stethoscope you can still sometimes hear a little *murmur*.

One of the last things the cardiologist said to my parents when he signed me off – we were all there, (my sister as well), was – *buy this one a football, but get a cap and gown for Simone*. It was a carelessly offered comment, meant jovially, but in a way it determined the way our childhoods would progress, my sister encouraged to be practical and physical, *including the ballet lessons*, whereas there was for me, a level of academic expectation and anxious watchfulness. My sister confounded her prediction and did go to university. She was *a late starter* but has achieved much, and continues to do so.

Instead of ballet, I had singing and elocution lessons – maybe there was a trace of a Welsh accent to be eradicated. Maybe these were considered suitable hobbies for the less active one. I was painfully shy and all the exams and competitions I was channelled towards were a torture. Yet, all the songs and speeches and poems I had to learn confirmed my love of words, of the spoken and sung word in particular.

*

44

In convent number three there was a girl with six fingers. The sixth finger was a fairly useless adjunct to the fifth, but an object of fascination to the rest of us. She was an excellent swimmer and, when we were all picnicking at the outdoor swimming pool in Wokingham, her other USP was eating apples and pears in their entirety, including the pips and cores. That outdoor pool is long gone. It had been gifted to the town early in the twentieth century for the benefit of the town. It was sold off to property developers.

Polydactyly has been associated either with luck or with misfortune, with being privileged or being cursed. Anne Boleyn's polydactyly, which may actually just have been an extra fingernail, was used as supporting evidence for her accusers. Poor Anne.

*

When I was twenty-four and living in Bristol I studied to achieve my Speech and Drama teaching qualification. I had done my EFL training a couple of years before, got married and had a baby. The Speech and Drama certificate was not really intended to be vocational: it was just the last, highest exam, so needed to be ticked off my list. I walked to Clifton from Cotham once or twice a week, pushing the buggy, for a lesson with Elizabeth. She was a kind and inspirational woman who sadly died of a heart attack not long afterwards. Theory was the hardest element and there, mnemonics helped, like the one for the metrical feet - *Iambus comes with heavy pace,* which includes the line – *next comes the dactyl on pattering feet...*

*

Unlike my boys, and I'm including the husband here as well, I have little physical courage, less appetite for physical risk and zero aptitude. Unlike them, I've had very few accidents resulting in the breaking of bones. There was a broken thumb when I stood on a kitchen chair to water a hanging basket outside the front door. I still had to stretch and somehow got my thumb caught in the metal chain. Slightly stunned and covered in hanging basket, chain, plants, earth, watering can and chair, I had to wait for assistance from the crowd of children indoors – mine plus all the neighbours' children – who were glued to their afternoon fix of *Neighbours*. The second breakage was a wrist, caused by tripping over rubble by the kitchen door about four years ago, and the third one was much more recently when a donkey bolted dragging me with it. It was ribs this time.

*

The husband, though, is digitally challenged. In the spring of 2000, he lost parts of three fingers on his right hand, in an unpleasantly close encounter with his motorbike. I will never forget his white face, the bleeding – the white goods in our utility room sprayed with thin arcs of red, and my frantic scrabbling in the dirt for the missing bits.

A year or so ago, he caught his left thumb in a log splitter and removed the tip of it. I have told him not to do it again.

*

My elder son broke his foot badly when he was twenty, a climbing escapade up the side of a multi-storey car park which went badly wrong. Mountaineering efforts were preceded by the consumption of alcohol. His foot turned one hundred and eighty degrees. That foot now has a titanium ball, to add to his other bionic elements.

*

My youngest child – who has been much less accident prone than the males of our family - cut her foot badly at a sixth form party. The timing of it was awful, so close to her exams…

She had been dancing barefoot in a village hall. There was broken glass. After a skin graft or two, her foot slowly healed, but the dressing had to be changed at a local hospital every day. Generally, I took her to these appointments, but, on one occasion, the husband did the trip. He spun the car and ended in a ditch.

He was going through – I suppose – a mid-life crisis period of driving recklessness. He had bought a crazy car, and he grew horns and a tail when behind the wheel. It lasted for about a year during which time he also had a one month ban for speeding. I have not often been angry, really angry with him, but he'd put our daughter in danger too. I was incandescent with rage.

46

I mentioned the donkeys, our noisy, expensive, long-eared follies of the last eleven years. The most expensive aspect of donkey maintenance is foot care. Their hooves need trimming regularly every six or seven weeks by a farrier. It is not an occupation which has never tempted me.

With our two asses, it is always a battle of wits and a hazardous exercise. They do not enjoy the process. The smaller one, who is less food-driven, is harder to bribe and distract. With her, a constant state of vigilance is essential. I am still building up confidence slowly since the bolting incident a year ago. But did I say how wonderful their ears smell? I so get Titania's infatuation.

Fabric

It's a stand-off. One woman, one girl. Mother and daughter. And it's about clothes, more precisely, what the girl is going to wear to a dance at the boys' school. She's had to be persuaded to go anyway. She's sure it's not her thing and that she'll have a ghastly time.

And now she'll be a laughingstock, the butt of jokes, because 'Mummy' won't let her wear black velvet. Everyone's chosen outfit for this event is a black velvet mini dress bought from one of two chain stores in Reading. For once, everyone really is everyone. Or nearly. Her schoolmates will be distinguished by what they're wearing on their feet, or the colour and length of their hair. Black velvet is really some sort of uniform.

Of course, I was too busy smarting at my failure, the unreasonableness of my ridiculously old-fashioned mother, to see anything good in being different. My mother made me a nut-brown velvet dress, a mini like the others, long sleeved like the others, with a lace collar and cuffs just like the others. My lace was cream not white; my velvet was thicker and better quality. I hated that dress.

'Young girls, under the age of eighteen, do not wear black velvet.'

*

The dance was so-so, despite my perceived humiliation, and the hideous shyness I was afflicted with. I met a boy, a boarder, who seemed as awkward and uneasy as I was. He asked me to write to him. I did. Though I think I was unkind to him later.

*

Years afterwards, when packing to go to uni, I found the dress, crumpled on the floor of the wardrobe. Mum had obviously spent time and effort in its making. It was actually gorgeous. But I never wore it again and I never got round to thanking her.

We didn't talk much anymore. Easy companionship had gone. It was my father's good opinion I cared about. My sister talked to Mum, talked and fought, pushing the boundaries.

Clothes remained one of the few incendiary topics for Mum and me. She liked quality and believed, rightly or wrongly, that mass-produced clothes were badly made and a false economy. She made quite a few of our dresses, but I recall a dressmaker when I was young who sometimes made summer clothes for us all. And then a tailor we went to later, when we'd started to receive parcels from the aunt who worked for that very genteel charity. Again, this is all rather baffling, as, in so many other ways, we were scrimping and penny-pinching...

*

My mother had a Singer sewing machine with a treadle, lovely as a machine, lovely as a piece of furniture. Watching her working at it made me think of trying to pat my head with one hand while tracing circles on my belly with the other. Not something I would ever master. Mum was almost, but not quite, as skilled as her sister at dressmaking, knitting, quilting, rug-making – all the crafts requiring needles. Her sister had much more time though.

My uncle gave me a knitting Nancy – French knitting it was called – and I briefly found the making of long useless woollen cords quite soothing. Very occasionally, I was allowed to help my mother and sister make rugs, the sort where you use a metal hook to pull loops of wool through canvas. It was never for long. The women in my family lost patience with my clumsiness and left-handedness.

Besides, books were so much more satisfying.

*

There was another fight, this time about bright orange tights and a very short turquoise cord mini dress. It had short sleeves, a stand-up collar and a long front zip. Mum thought it was a silly purchase, cheap throwaway fashion. It was of course, but then needlecord is almost as

49

tactile as velvet. I loved the feel and the look of it, and wore it till it fell apart. Alas, far too soon.

I wore this dress for the first time for a double date, a blind date…to the cinema. The film was an 'X', violent and misogynistic. The story was incomprehensible, but then I missed chunks of it while fending off the mouth and hands of the unappealing boy I'd been set up with. I was underage and besieged. The dress was fab though.

*

The few wedding pictures I've seen of Mum and Dad's wedding are in black and white. Fewer than twenty people attended. She and my father look happy and excited, as does her sister.

Everyone else looks severe, dour, even grumpy. Her dress is just below knee length, pale blue velvet. She told me the choice of style and fabric was based on what was available. In truth, she loved tactile fabrics too.

She wouldn't have worn white anyway, even though she told me it suited her darker, (more like my sister's), colouring. Cream suited me better she felt. In her code of sartorial rules, white could only be worn by virgins.

*

My aunt used to make trips up to London at the end of 'the season' and buy up rolls of fabric from fashion houses. They would *come in useful* one day. Long before she married, she went to the closing down sale of a major fashion house, and bought yards of Chinese ivory silk brocade, and yards of delicate lacey veil material. This was intended, not for herself or for her sister, but for the daughter she hoped she'd have one day. It came to me, as her elder niece.

A dear and skilled friend made my wedding dress. I lost touch with her decades ago, without ever really expressing that I appreciated what she'd done for me. The fabric was over thirty years old by the time of my wedding. It was intricate, elegant, smooth and beautiful, (as it is still: I have kept the dress.) I was traditional in many ways – my uni friends and acquaintances were mostly opining that marriage was outmoded, and that there was no way they would succumb. Definitely not until they were *really old*. But wearing a veil seemed too retro, too patriarchal even to me. I wanted security; the loss of my mother had cast me adrift in ways I didn't understand at the time. However, sacrificial lamb wasn't going to be on the sartorial menu that wedding day. I casually, and probably gracelessly, rejected this other roll of flimsy stuff. This bride was *not* going to wear a veil.

The aunt who gave me my wedding dress material died, unexpectedly, nine years after I married. She was neither old nor ill. You always assume there'll be plenty of time to say thank you, plenty of time to say sorry. But it isn't so.

Flowers

On my wedding morning, very early, I rode pillion on the groom's Triumph, from N8 to Covent Garden, to buy apricot, orange, peach and cream flowers. There were to be three posies, handmade by us of course, for me and the two bridesmaids – my schoolfriend from convent number three and my nineteen year old sister. It was to be a brown and cream DIY wedding, befitting the times and our very limited resources.

*

I've always hated being told not to send flowers. It's one of the things you can do to show sympathy, to feel like you're sharing in the grief. Wearing black or wearing whatever those closest to the departed ask you to do, makes you feel like you're doing something.

We were told to wear something green. The coffin was green wicker. My sister ordered the flowers for which her family and mine would split the cost. She was outraged, appalled, horrified by what the florists created. I've only just discovered why. Purple flowers, lots of greenery and then some white arum lilies to fill in the gaps. Apparently the design didn't work; apparently the lilies were too big, out-of-scale with the rest of the arrangement. I didn't notice. If I noticed anything it was that yes, we had sent flowers and yes, weren't these the suffragette colours – purple, green and white?

The deceased was the younger daughter of my mum's Irish friend from Tenby. She hadn't made it to her three score and ten. We didn't know her as well as her older sister, who had lived with us for a while when she was in her teens. We never knew what to call the relationship – daughters of a family friend hadn't quite covered it.

Sometimes I'd call the older sibling a cousin, or a foster sister. There wasn't really a term for the bond between us, between our families.

*

When I moved to Bristol with the husband, it was quite a lonely existence. His colleagues at work were young but mostly unmarried, and none of them had children. We were the only couple in our circle of friends who had started breeding. My uni friends were generally unattached, or rabidly feminist and hungry for their careers. We didn't really fit in anywhere.

I started going to mother and baby groups which were run by vicars' wives. I had a friend I'd made at ante-natal classes and then two friends who were vicars' wives. One of them was married to an older man who climbed and was into motorbikes – so, despite the dog collar, he and the husband got on well too. This second vicar's wife died relatively young, of a brain tumour. I received a message just as we returned from a Greek holiday. We were told not to send flowers. No fuss. Charitable donations only. I wanted to scream.

*

Because of the businesses we've run, we've been at the beginning of lots of people's adult lives, the beginning of many careers. One of our proteges came to our home for an interview when he was twenty-four. Easy on the eye, with much potential but thus far directionless.

We offered him a job on the spot and he went off to a local bar, to celebrate. Where he met his future wife, a sophisticated lady a few years his senior. He always felt he'd scored the jackpot with her. He was renowned for the lavish gifts he chose for her, for birthdays, Christmas, Valentine's Day and anniversaries. One of them was a year's subscription to a floristry service. Fresh flowers would be delivered to his ladylove once a fortnight for a year. I had no idea this was 'a thing' and that anyone I knew would ever make such an extravagant, romantic gesture. There were fleeting thoughts about waste and the environment, but these faded. I actually thought - *Lucky woman!*

53

Fancy dress

The woman climbing towards us, over the backs of the red velveteen theatre seats, was long of limb and white of teeth. She was dressed in an outdoorsy, sporty style and was obviously both affluent and American. She was Mary Tyler Moore, a huge star in my youth.

We had taken our little girl to the theatre. It was a Noel Coward play, possibly too old for her, but she revelled in the sense of occasion anyway. It was an opportunity to put on her bridesmaid outfit from two years before, the shepherdess style Laura Ashley number she'd worn to my sister's wedding. In the two summers since, she'd had a growth spurt and this was to be absolutely the last time she was able to squeeze into that dress.

The ingenue in that production was Sara Crowe, of Philadelphia cheese advert fame, later to become the first, blushing and gushing, bride in *Four Weddings and a Funeral*.

*

I couldn't sew, so dressing up requirements at school were fulfilled, on a wing and a prayer, by charity shop finds, cutting, tearing, sticking, pinning and tying. Somehow, I just about got away with it. One of my favourite pictures of the children is of them, in an assortment of green, rust and brown rags, dressed in the characters of Robin Hood, Will Scarlet and Maid Marian. In the same unskilled manner, I just about managed ghosts, clowns and Cinderella. There was never any thought of buying a Disney character costume – they must have existed. I guess it would have been thought of as cheating.

*

I have no memories of dressing up as a child except being a pink powder puff in the carnival when I was about six – lots of cotton wool balls and a borrowed tutu and ballet shoes. This was an exquisite joy for me as I was not allowed to learn ballet, unlike my younger sister. Then there was a school production of *Wind in the Willows*. I was an eleven-year-old baby boy rabbit wearing checked shorts with a large white pompom on my bottom. This was a less than exquisite experience.

*

Fancy dress passed me by throughout my adolescence and then, from my mid-twenties onwards, it was a sporadic occurrence. My sister had a Halloween party just after the second baby was born and I borrowed my mother-in-law's black yoga leotard, fashioned rudimentary whiskers, ears and tail and went as a witch's cat. *Wild horses* have never, and would never, persuade me to wear anything quite so revealing to a party again.

There were two work parties I remember when we hired costumes in desperation. One we were going to go dressed as Good Queen Bess and Walter Raleigh. The costumes were heavy and scratchy, abandoned at the last minute for something cobbled together – schoolboy and schoolgirl. Mine was loosely based on St. Trinian's. Someone I was dancing with grabbed my nipples through my school blouse and pulled hard. He was the older brother of one of our employees. It hurt. I stopped dancing with him.

Another work party was memorable for all the wrong reasons. It was a Victorian evening and one of our colleagues, a broad stocky man with a large stomach, well over six feet tall, had hired an elaborate Queen Victoria costume. He was a man the husband had a short-lived side business venture with, with two other computer geeky types. For some unfathomable reason, Queen Victoria decided to do a striptease. I left the room when he got down to his speedo sized underpants and never looked at him in quite the same light again.

*

And then, just after I came back to Wales, we went to Goodwood and I hired a 1940s costume. I did not take the uneven ground, lots of walking and warm weather into consideration. The fabrics were synthetic. I flushed, perspired, sweltered and the heels gave me blisters.

Themed parties and murder mysteries abounded from when I was in my late thirties. Some where you were given props at the door, and maybe a character to play too, others where you knew in advance who you were playing, so arrived in costume. At one of these latter events I was a hard-drinking, extremely fierce riding instructress. I embraced both the character and the drinking a little too well, was not well and was carried in a fireman's lift out to the car. Not my finest moment.

*

Both sons sang as little and not quite so little boys. Every Sunday they donned cassocks and ruffs and played the angelic choirboy. There was an occasional pound to be made by singing at weddings on a Saturday too. At my sister's wedding, my elder son sang *Ave Maria*. His voice broke within days of his solo. His younger brother's role was as *usher*, dressed in top hat and tails, looking like a rather smarter version of the Artful Dodger.

Both boys dabbled a little in theatricals at a local arts centre. The elder was in *James and the Giant Peach* and a couple of pantos. The younger was in *Tosca*. These appearances required performing licences from the local authority. At many of these performances, I gained a little extra part-time work as a *theatre mummy*, backstage with the child performers, making sure they didn't make too much noise, arrived on stage at the right time and in the right costumes, etc. Despite the presence of one or two little divas, most of the time it was great fun. I made up word searches, read stories and generally tried to keep them calm. We wanted all the energy and enthusiasm on stage, not spent before they left the dressing room.

I was extremely grateful to be employed at one of the pantos. The star was a performer who had known better, more famous, times. He was probably in his early fifties, but well preserved and with an indefatigable sense of his own magnetism. He gazed longingly at most of the girls, a few of the prettier boys and attempted to fumble me in the wings. It was necessary to keep an eye on him. I felt my role that Christmas was more of a civic duty.

Ferries, and things which mostly float

The thought has crossed my mind that, if given the choice, I'd rather be in a *boat disaster*, than stuck underground or in a plane crash. I'm very slightly claustrophobic. Never got in the way of a childhood game of sardines, but it did make itself apparent – the claustrophobia, that is – when we went to Cheddar Gorge. I was about six or seven months pregnant with my first, carrying it all before me, centre of gravity seriously modified. My blood pressure was a bit low too! As we descended and the air began to change, a feeling of apprehension gathered momentum inside me. Not far from the bottom I passed out. A couple of serendipitous German tourists carried me up to the surface.

Many summers after this, we were Eurocamping with the children in Southern France and visited caves with them twice; once to have a glimpse of the Roquefort cheesemaking process, once to see fantastic formations of stalagmites and stalactites. On both occasions I was conscious of fear but held it together.

*

After the *mites* grew and the *tites* started to respond to the inevitability of gravity, we went on a sailing holiday, just once, for a week, with my sister-in-law and her husband. It was in the Ionian and should have been idyllic. I love the water and love islands even more. However, (our berths below deck, whether bow or stern I have no recollection), had very limited headroom and were hot and airless. Because I'm smaller than my husband, and out of years of habit, I chose the inside slot, with even less space above me, and even further away from any possibility of fresh air or a breeze. There was little sleep for the week, despite my best efforts at counting imaginary fluffy things and self-medicating with local wine. I imagine being buried alive in a white fibreglass coffin must be similar.

*

For a few years, I was teaching part-time and he was working for an

American company. We had left Bristol for Berkshire. Having briefly sold his architectural soul for some welcome pieces of silver, he achieved membership of the 100% club, or 110% club, or something like that. He was invited to an island off the coast of North Carolina with two or three British colleagues. Wives went along too. My in-laws babysat. I think it was my first time of visiting the US.

The trip was nominally a conference, but mostly it was about team-bonding, mutual self-congratulation and eating. I had never experienced such humidity. Air conditioning inside the hotel complex was set so high, that sunglasses steamed up as soon as we emerged. There was no possibility of taking photographs. I am fair-skinned and not a serious poolside sun-baster. I also have a low boredom threshold. All the women were offered a complimentary massage, and each guest had a gift on arrival – a copy of Jonathan Livingstone Seagull. This is not a long book. My husband, an adventurous soul, decided to provide entertainment for us one afternoon, to while away a couple of hours before dinner. It was cooler that day, blueness interrupted by a few clouds on the horizon. Despite being advised against it - or, if we were determined to go ahead, to make it a very brief foray – we took out a catamaran.

I hadn't been on one before. Though I'd once been on a glass-bottomed boat, where you can see the water below. This was somewhat different. There *were* moments where exhilaration overcame my terror. They were few and infrequent. The wind strengthened. Clouds gathered and mustered and turned an unpleasant shade of dark gunmetal. It began to rain and rain heavily. The husband struggled to get us back to shore. He didn't admit this, but it was pretty obvious, even to a non-sailor like myself. Dinner that evening was accompanied by sounds of rain, not a polite British summer downpour, but something altogether more violent.

*

We all know about the Titanic. We all remember catastrophic ferry disasters too. Yet I always, despite that catamaran and the Ionian yacht, feel safe and happy on a boat. And being on a ferry crossing, from one piece of land to another, *never* palls. It doesn't matter if the

59

crossing lasts fifteen minutes or many hours. They all thrill me. Especially if the crossing is to an island!

*

In the Summer of 1970, I wept at the port. Eventually, someone took pity on me and let me onto the ferry back to Portsmouth without payment. I had been robbed and let down. The significance of that festival was overshadowed by what had happened. I was definitely not going to trust a boy, any boy, *ever* again. When we docked, my father picked me up after a short wait. I had reversed the phone charges. He didn't ask any questions on our drive back. I slept for about twenty hours. Like a baby.

*

The summer before my daughter married, we were at a different wedding, in South Devon. The bride was, (and is), a granddaughter of my mother's Irish friend from Tenby. The bride looked beautiful; her mother looked elegant; the weather was kind. The next day we went to the art deco Burgh Island Hotel for lunch, a minute rocky landmass next to Bigbury-on-Sea. No ferry is needed to reach the island. Access is by a tall, strange-looking tractor or on foot. We took our shoes off and padded with happy anticipation across the sand. Burgh Island had been on my island list for years. It was a spectacular afternoon.

Another wedding, a couple of summers before and we did travel by ferry for almost every day from the island venue to Rovinj, in Istria, Northern Croatia and back again. A good friend and former colleague was marrying a Croatian woman. The stretch of water between the town and the hotel was calm, blue and welcoming but, just after the outside ceremony, there was a dramatic, unexpected thunderstorm. It was short-lived. Festivities and spirits were undampened.

We spent a blissful, welcome and necessary two weeks of downtime. We came back to the farm to an altogether different ambience. Unbeknownst to my daughter-in-law, the residential group who had just left, had been taking part in a couples therapy course. Sexual therapy. Housekeeping staff were feeling the strain. They

60

called it tantric, but the frolicking had left grass stains on duvets and oily footprints on the walls.

*

There was an odd gurgling sound I couldn't identify. It was a four berth cabin and we were a family of five. We were crossing to Denmark. Legoland was beckoning.

I'd volunteered to sleep on the floor. I'm not sure why. Maybe the husband's back was playing up. Whatever the reason, everyone else was tucked up, asleep, in their single berths, with webbing straps secured lest it was a rough night at sea. I didn't expect to drop off, but I dozed fitfully. The gurgling woke me. I collected myself together, cursing the noisy pipes. But the noise wasn't plumbing.

It was my eldest. Like me, he's a restless sleeper, a tosser and a turner. He must have rolled over several times and now the webbing straps were wrapped tightly round his neck. He was choking. I released him, quite possibly *in the nick of time*. Drama over, the cabin resumed its collective slumbers.

For the hours which remained till morning, I was on full alert, wide awake, grateful for the uncomfortable floor and for my bad night's sleep.

*

I have reached islands by plane, by causeway or bridge, across the sand at low tide, and, of course, by ferry. My first must have been Caldey, just off the coast from Tenby, when I was very young. My second, the Isle of Wight. I started counting the ones I'd visited and stopped between thirty and forty – there are many more, around the British Isles and further, that I hope to visit.

The ones furthest away ones we probably won't travel to. Neither I nor my husband can justify long-haul flights anymore. Our world has become far too fragile. But that still leaves plenty of islands we can still reach, and will reach, by ferry.

61

Fame and fortune

Some of my schoolfriends had autograph books. It was a thing back then. One contemporary, an only child who lived in a Victorian house on the outskirts of Reading, had three interests – shopping, tennis and famous people. Her mother gave her a large amount of freedom, provided that she was always accompanied by a *nice, sensible girl*. For a while, I must have satisfied all of these criteria.

I trailed after her to tennis tournaments, where she hovered before and after the event, autograph book and pen thrust out optimistically, hoping to meet one of her heroes or heroines. It was never Wimbledon, but then tennis isn't all about SW19. I hovered too, a shorter, less enthusiastic minder, barely able to identify these white-clad Gods.

We also went to London every couple of months, by train on a Saturday when I wasn't working, to wander around Kensington High Street, Carnaby Street, Oxford Street and so on. I had enough funds for the fare, a lunch of tomato soup, a roll, and a coffee. I didn't much like the taste of coffee but was trying to acquire it. My friend liked the perfume counters in department stores. She had proper grown-up perfume with French names, like Ma Griffe and Chanel No. 5. My nose was less sophisticated by far. We ambled around markets and lurked in Biba. She bought an Afghan coat, which didn't suit her. She pointed out people who might have been, or looked like, celebrities. Once she thought she saw Patti Boyd; once there was someone who looked like Marianne Faithfull. I knew who Marianne Faithfull was. Many of the girls at my third convent went on to St. Joseph's, aka *Holy Jo's*, in Reading, when they reached eleven. She was an ex-pupil of Holy Jo's who was now famous, even notorious. I also had a much-played copy of her *'As Tears Go By'.*

When we were fourteen or fifteen, my friend dragged me along to a lecture about Eastern mysticism and meditation. She signed up for a course. I wasn't keen on the scent of joss sticks, and was unimpressed by both the *guru* and the experience. We drifted further apart, she into an odd combination of privileged consumerism and the road to enlightenment; me, into poetry, love, academic confusion and a bout of teenage mental instability.

*

Years before, in June 1962, the Queen and Prince Philip had come to Wokingham. I don't know what prompted the visit. It was a big occasion though, with views about royalty being less complicated, less conflicted than now. Full summer uniform was obligatory for us convent girls. Hats, blazers, our rather stylish French-designed summer dresses, polished shoes, white ankle socks and white gloves.

We were all inspected before we were allowed to walk crocodile fashion, into the centre of town and find a place to wait. There was a long wait. Eventually the Rolls Royce – I think it was a Rolls - appeared and we all waved our flags. It was over in seconds.

*

Many years later we were in London. The children were off school for the day. The two boys, scrubbed, brushed, cassocked and ruffed, were part of a choir assembled to sing for the Queen Mother's ninetieth birthday. There were events throughout the day and we had packed a picnic. At one point we were waiting, behind some sort of barrier, with a heavy but jovial police presence, and we were clapping a group of runners. There was a former boxer was in the group; his presence had once been ubiquitous, now much less so. We thought he looked directly at us and that his eyes seemed sad.

*

Fan clubs proliferated. I was, for a short time, a member of The Man from U.N.C.L.E. club and some sort of road safety group. Involving squirrels I think. We all loved *Blue Peter,* even though my crafting

63

attempts were doomed to failure. I went alone to a fete which was being opened by a *Blue Peter* presenter, John Noakes, and his dog. I was ecstatic to be able to stroke the dog but no, did not ask for either an autograph or a pawprint.

*

When the husband had worked for the American company for a couple of years, the company who'd provided us with a *holiday* in North Carolina, he was invited to join two other men in a new venture. There would be three of them, an M.D, a sales guy and himself, the approachable face of technology. It was *meant to be* an equal partnership.

The husband was excited by the challenge and threw himself into it. He worked long hours. He was committed to his clients. He was less interested in flash cars, fancy restaurants and the whole culture of showing off than the others were.

Out of work hours, and there weren't many of these, we ran a church youth club together. The children were growing busier and needed constant ferrying. Life was full. Gradually, the differences between the priorities of the three men became a source of irritation. With anger, disappointment and a degree of bitterness following soon afterwards. The M.D. had become *the boss*, living an extravagant lifestyle, spending huge amounts, unchecked and uncheckable.

Once we went to a Michelin starred restaurant by the river in Bray – the three supposed *partners* and their wives-stroke-girlfriends. *We* weren't looking forward to it, not imagining there would be much for vegetarians to eat. As it happened, we were pleasantly surprised.

The next table was ringed by a number of very well-built, stocky *waiters*, awkwardly squeezed into their uniforms. At that table, just about visible, were Prince Andrew and Fergie, and their dinner companions, a fashionable society interior designer and her musician husband. They seemed to be enjoying themselves. The M.D. felt it was appropriate to *send over* a very expensive bottle of champagne to our neighbours. *We* were mortified.

The company the husband and I had started together in late 1990

64

outgrew our early nineteenth century house by the roundabout. We converted the buildings tacked on the side into a two-storey office. Even as the builders finished the conversion, we were outgrowing the space.

If the children were at home, I tried to keep them quiet and out of the way when important customers came for meetings. No washing on the line either. I'm sure foreign visitors knew we lived *above the shop*, but they were far too polite to mention it, and our business expanded. We moved to new premises, rented space in converted farm buildings outside Maidenhead. It was almost countryside, flat farming land, wide vistas, with the River Thames close and the M4 closer.

*

The millennium approached. There was feverish expectation about what would happen when the clocks struck midnight on December 31st 1999. Vast amounts were spent trying to avert the anticipated computer chaos. The bug. But nothing happened.

We were named one of Tony Blair's millennium businesses. I presume there were 2000 of us, but possibly it was just 1000. The award was for design and innovation. We, the husband, our top technical guru and me, were invited to Tower Bridge at dawn. It was a freezing morning. Suited, booted and shivering, we were taken down the river to the new Millennium Dome. Tony Blair made a speech. The rows of seats were steeply banked. He was a very small figure in the distance. There were nibbles, a modicum of warm fizz and some sort of commemorative award.

*

There was another prize, this time just a local small business award. Far less *hoopla*, but the local MP, a certain Mrs May, presented it to us in our office. This meant the whole team could take part, plus it happened at a much more civilised hour. I remember noting what a tall woman she is and how genuinely interested she seemed to be in what we did. I was concerned she might bump her head on our barn's low beams. I noticed the splendid shoes too.

*

We entertained customers a lot. Round the corner from the office was a pub-cum-restaurant owned by Michael Parkinson. The walls were lined with autographed photos of the famous people he'd interviewed. That was amusement in itself, spotting images of the great, the good and the entertaining-but-not-quite-so-good. Foreign clients loved it when we took them there for lunch. On Fridays, Mrs Parkinson sometimes popped in with crisp, clean tablecloths – red and white checked ones I think. Occasionally, the man himself could be spotted propping up the bar.

Another place we took visitors to was a local arts centre, which regularly put on lunchtime shows, try-outs for future runs elsewhere. Once we took a group from a Dutch airline for a half an hour intimate show where Lenny Henry was trying out new material. I know what you're going to ask – the level of English of almost all our European customers was fantastic…and much humour is universal anyway.

One of the special treats we laid on for foreign clients was a traditional English afternoon tea on Monkey Island, preceded by a trip down the Thames on an Edwardian boat, pointing out the houses of celebrities – some no longer with us, like Paul Daniels, the magician; some now no longer with us for other reasons, like a certain multi-talented popular Australian performer and artist. I suppose it was the River Thames equivalent of the bus tour past the homes of stars in Beverley Hills. I went on that once. It was very nearly a disaster, but that's for another time.

Fragile

It was a rare break, a week on the Amalfi coast. We were always travelling. Most trips, if they could be defined as holiday at all, were a day or two stuck on to the end of a business trip, or a trade show. Or if he was travelling alone, then I might fly out to join him for a couple of days at the end of meetings. This was meant to be *seven work-free days*.

On the way out, we ended up at the back of business class. No idea how. Small plane, small cabin. In the front row was a then very famous English model-cum-actress and her extremely wealthy fiancé. Gossip mags were full of stories about their engagement. I remember her long tanned legs extended up the cabin wall, her bare feet, her multi-storey make-up case – weren't they called vanity cases once? This was more of a vanity trunk, a seriously impressive piece of kit, which looked much too large to be *carry-on*. I remember the very loud argument which ensued. Raised voices resounded around the cabin. We all pretended we weren't listening.

On one of the days we took the trip to Capri, where we saw the uber-glamorous couple, both dressed completely in white, just leaving the island by private charter boat to return to the mainland.

We were on the same flight home with them as well, a quieter trip. Their wedding did eventually happen about three years later but I guess their relationship must have been *fragile*. The marriage was over within three years.

*

There *were* lovely times in that week. We struck up a holiday friendship with another couple and ate with them most evenings, after a limoncello or two in the bar opposite. He was the man who had a patent for inventing glass chopping boards, (you know, the ones which make a horrible scratching noise), and his idea had served them well financially.

*

I have always loved green glass, usually decorative rather than useful. We were always breaking glasses at home and there were never any matching ones. There was a corner shop, in Amalfi or Praiano, with dark green second-hand glass goblets on display in the window. They weren't expensive. We bought twelve or them, six in each size, and wrapped them in newspapers, towels and clothes for the homebound journey. Alas, the case containing the carefully wrapped glasses must have been the one the porters selected to drop, throw or kick onto the tarmac. All bar two glasses smashed. Now, only one remains.

Another fragile purchase came from Ravello. On our first visit, we bought three pieces of brightly glazed kitchen ceramics, a large jug and two bowls. All survived. All are still used. In the shop where we bought them, the lady who was serving us was in the midst of wrapping up and packing a huge ornate black and gold dinner service. It was being collected later that day. The purchaser was Cliff Richard.

*

We were constantly being reminded of our own mortality that week, in Pompeii and then again every time we were on one of those picturesque coastal roads which cling to the edge of the Mediterranean. The second trip to Ravello was on a little scooter we'd hired. We'd seen a poster about an outdoor recital. We thought it would be a fabulously romantic evening setting for classical music. It was. But we felt more than a little vulnerable on the cliff road back later that night.

*

Work crept in. The holiday was interrupted again and again, albeit with polite apologies. There were messages and phone calls. We argued about boundaries, argued about promises, argued about work-life balance. When the fighting stopped, there was an uneasy, brittle peace.

Something had changed, but ultimately we came through this, as we have so many other things. What shattered that time was our business. It had been a struggle since 9/11. The pressure was unsustainable. We had to sell up the following year. And in amongst all the other strains, the glass on the family portrait was crazing. One of our children was heading for his first crisis.

*

I heard a radio programme once. The guy was speaking about his own mental health. He mentioned the San Andreas fault in California. It's about 750 miles long. Each of the three segments has different characteristics and each has different degrees of risk. Millions of people live in places where they could be seriously affected by earthquakes.

I think he was saying that most, if not all of us, have demons, weak spots, pressure points. Many of us live with fault lines in our brain chemistry. Most of us will muddle through, relatively unscathed. A few tremors. No serious damage. But a few of us of will be there, in the wrong place, at the wrong time, when all hell breaks loose. And whether that's you, or me, or your child, or my child, is all a matter of luck and timing.

Family and fireworks

I am so disappointed with my DNA results!

Apparently, I'm 43 per cent English, 37 per cent of which comes from my mother. From her I also get my 10 per cent of Scottish DNA, 2 per cent from Norway and 1 per cent from Sweden and Denmark.

From my father, there is no Scandinavian blood. Instead I am 3 per cent French, 2 per cent Irish and there's that rogue 6 per cent of English DNA I get from him. I'm also 39 per cent Welsh. That's all.

My sister, who is deeply involved in tracing both sides of our family, has a subtly different profile. More Welsh for starters. I don't understand the science but feel *cheated* by my DNA.

For years, after I left Wales as a child, I would feel *hiraeth*, (that untranslatable sense of homesickness, longing, yearning, wistfulness and nostalgia), without ever knowing that the word existed. For years, decades, until we settled in Wales in early 2007, my heart would race, ever so slightly, as I crossed the Severn Bridge in a westerly direction. When we moved to the farm, it felt like coming home.

My dad was born in Wales; his father had farmed here; his family lived here. I was born here. *Where had my 50% Welshness gone?* Sure – if you add on the Scottish and Irish elements, then I am just over 50% *Celtic* – but has someone made a mistake? How accurate are these things anyway?

*

My sister's genealogical discoveries are extensive, thorough and ongoing. In our ancestors over the last four hundred years we number

70

paupers, peasants, tenant farmers, criminals, skilled craftspeople, self-made men and women too, politicians, mayors, soldiers, sailors, doctors, nurses, clergymen, landowners, at least one possible slave trader, musicians, publicans, engineers, a writer or two, translators, teachers, suffragists and two Gunpowder Plotters.

In education, wealth, occupation and social status we have spanned the spectrum. In death as in life. My ancestors have died in their beds, on the battlefield, at sea, in childbirth, in tuberculosis sanatoriums, in the workhouse and on the gallows. My forebears, it would seem, have been an eclectic bunch.

*

I am ambivalent about November 5th. As a student in Brighton, it was *de rigueur* to attend the Bonfire Night festivities in the neighbouring town of Lewes. At least once. Without knowing anything then of the Papist Wynter brothers I am connected to, the Lewes *celebrations* appalled me. Traditional, yes, but only a breath, a toxic breath, from barbarism. I am not proud of the plotters, but remain appalled at how they died, and the cruelty involved. Hanging, drawing and quartering. And apparently, the real story is more complex, more nuanced, than the Guy Fawkes tales we were taught at school.

*

I once got off a train at Brighton Station to be met by a bomb scare. It was a busy time of day. The announcement told us not to panic, to exit in an calm, orderly fashion. Everyone ran as if their lives depended on it. No one knew it wasn't a real bomb.

*

We were in Atlanta, by the airport, on September 11th. The inviolate was violated. There was disbelief after the devastation and then the sky was silenced. Flights stopped. We wanted to go home but couldn't. There were candlelit vigils. Sales of GodBlessAmerica tee-shirts, and guns, boomed.

It was heartbreakingly sad, but disaster - extreme, unexpected disaster – draws people together. In some, it brings out the best -

71

bravery, compassion, kindness and generosity. We were in the hotel bar, watching visceral grief and useless commentary on the mammoth screens. A man wanted to buy us drinks, because we were British. *'Nuke the bastards,'* he said. We could sense what was coming.

I abhor religious and ethnic intolerance. Violence, of course, too.

*

I would, I think, have been a suffragist and not a suffragette. Not for me the firebombs, the shattered glass, the King's horse. But we owe them all such a debt. Our lives were immeasurably changed for the better. The system's far from perfect, but I would *never* not vote.

*

There were relatives of my great, great grandmother – a Colonel Blathwayt, his wife and daughter. They lived at Eagle House near Bath. They supported suffragettes and suffragists. They supported them financially, emotionally and practically. There's was an open house, a welcoming space for women coming out of Holloway Prison, women who'd been on hunger strike, both *firebrand* leaders and their foot soldiers. Each woman was offered the chance to plant a tree in the grounds of Eagle House, a symbolic gesture of new birth, and hope for the future.

In the West, women are not chattels anymore. We have a voice. We have autonomy over our bodies, the right to choose – in theory at least. But progress is recent and fragile, and is being challenged elsewhere in the world, right now. Misogyny and bigotry are only just below the surface, sometimes barely that. Our freedoms are brittle. It could still all go up in flames again.

Fire and fumes

You're in the house. There are voices – chat and laughter – coming downstairs from the kitchen. And you're there, on the stairs, the last flight going past the loo on the half turn, leading just to your room and a couple of other small rooms, used just for storage.

Your bottom is on one of steps, not quite touching the brass stair-rod. You're holding onto two spindles, pressing your face between them, straining to hear the conversation drifting upwards. It's your mum and the friend who helps her, in the house and with the guests.

These women will stay close, even as the gap between them, geographical and emotional, widens over the next ten years or so. They'll stay close until the friend dies. Your mum will keep an eye on this woman's daughters, will offer a home to both – but only one of the prickly adolescents will accept. This girl will stay for a year or so. You will adore her, hero-worship her, but envy the easy bond she will have with both your parents. Your dad will be on standby at both girls' weddings, just in case their father fails to show. All this is a long way off. For now, it's two women working companionably. Shared gossip, confidences, laughter.

You strain to hear and find you've pushed your head, neck and part of her shoulders through the gaps. You're stuck. You freeze with fear. It's a long way down – forwards – to the hall floor. This has no carpet. You begin to wail.

I'm told this was the first time the fire brigade was called to rescue me. There were four times in total. How much was told to me? How much do I actually remember, or am I remembering what I was told? I was less than three, not much though. The second time, I was maybe a couple of months older – I recall late Spring, and my birthday is in March.

The second time wasn't in our house in Tenby, but on a cliff looking out across the beach to the sea. Again, I was stuck between railings. What was I doing? Who was with me? Why didn't they notice and stop me?

*

The next times happened after we left Wales, in the red-brick house which was home for ten years. There was a birthday party. Mine. We had a very basic toilet downstairs, at the end of a lean-to. It was a kind of potting shed-cum-sun room, with no element of leisure or luxury about it. It was rarely used, unless you were in the garden, and in a hurry. I took myself off to this dark, damp, spidery place to hide. I locked myself in and started to stuff Maltesers into my mouth. I was cross. I'd been given two boxes of those glorious chocolatey treats and had already *had* to open one of them that day, and share *nicely* with everyone. I was determined not to be cheated out of the second box. So I pulled the bolt and couldn't draw it back. I was locked in. I must have been about ten when the fire brigade came for the last time. This time it was actually for a fire. It was near to Christmas. My parents had left me alone, while they and my sister went up to the local shops to buy a few last-minute things. Brussels sprouts? Who knows? I decided to help tidy up. That was my justification.

The kitchen was full of piles of paper, old newspapers and magazines –two Sunday papers and at least one local paper were delivered every week. My mother had a monthly nursing magazine and the Woman's Weekly. My father took some radio ham publications and *The Exchange and Mart*. A monthly parish magazine popped through the letterbox too, even though we very, very rarely visited the local church.

I decided to reduce the clutter, to burn it. We'd have a clearer space for Christmas. I piled the papers into the range – all I can remember about it now was the circular, access hole at the top. I didn't put the lid down, just kept loading in the 'rubbish'. Flames leapt higher. Sparks caught and ignited the long wooden beam above the range. The kitchen filled with smoke.

Even if my intentions had been good, the results did not go down well with my parents. I had not achieved a clearer, tidier space for the

74

December festivities. I don't remember a punishment, shouting or reprisals. But there were white shocked faces. That was far worse.

*

An uncle by marriage was a fireman on the outskirts of London. He married my mum's sister. He was gregarious, funny, a lover of people in general and children in particular. He was full of energy and stories. When his little boy was diagnosed with leukaemia, he became a larger than life version of his avuncular self. There were a couple of huge lavish parties he and my aunt hosted during that time, with balloons, pin the tail on the donkey, professional entertainers, feasts and party games. It was what my uncle did – giving people a good time. He somehow hoped it might make my little cousin better. It didn't.

*

When my uncle retired from the fire service, he took a few more unusual part-time jobs. He modelled for a couple of advertising campaigns, for magazines and films. He acted as a regular extra for films and TV. He played the grizzled, characterful, uniformed older man – a postman, a chauffeur, a fisherman, a sailor.

*

The husband and I were in a minibus taxi late one night, returning from a party, a few years after we moved to West Wales. We were a group of eight or so, plus the driver. The conversation followed the usual routes. Where had we come from?

One woman was a great niece, or second cousin – something like that - of the Italian couple who had befriended my parents in Tenby all those years before. The female taxi driver had been to the same Berkshire convent as my younger sister, and we worked out that they'd played hockey or netball together – I forget which. The taxi driver's husband had been a fireman, from outer London, actually Bromley in Kent. He had been trained by my uncle. Degrees of separation? I couldn't have made it up, and it wouldn't have occurred to me to do so.

*

At least one of the advertising campaigns my uncle had been involved with was for the tobacco industry. Mum never smoked. My father was an awkward occasional smoker at family weddings. I saw him with a cigarette only a handful of times and he never looked as though he felt comfortable. Both my in-laws were heavy smokers. My mother-in-law contracted pneumonia several times in her sixties and early seventies. She suffered from asthma. My father-in-law had lung cancer in his seventies. They both gave up smoking after one of his lungs was removed.

*

The husband and I had given up smoking too, years before. I had smoked socially from when I was sixteen, heavily from when I went away to Brighton and then gave up when I became pregnant at twenty-three.

At uni, the smoking was part of the period look I intermittently aspired towards. My American friend bought me a black silver-tipped bakelite cigarette holder. I loved that thing. The second uni boyfriend broke it.

Both the husband and I drifted back into smoking for a while when the children were young. They would fine us mercilessly if they caught us. All of our children smoked. Just one does now I believe.

*

On the farm, where we were renting offices, there was a photographic studio. We sat for a rare family portrait, the five of us, meant to be a gift for my father-in-law when he was discharged from hospital. The photo was to remind him of how much we were concerned about him, singly and as a family unit. It was true – up to a point – we did care and we were all together that day. But the *smiles for Grandpa* concealed a more complex situation. Our eldest was unsettled, still a restless and reckless soul. Our middle child had hit the undergraduate jackpot of heartbreak and depression as he approached his final year. Our youngest, so biddable by comparison with her brothers when she was younger, was about to go off travelling with a boyfriend we weren't at all sure about. 9/11 would happen a couple of months afterwards, and we wouldn't know immediately how much our principal business, in the airline industry, would be impacted. And ultimately, how much *we* would be affected.

*

The next time all five of us would be together, brushed, washed and smartly dressed, would be at my father's funeral a year later.

Froggy and fishy

There was something highly fishy going on…

I didn't have anything to compare it with. I wasn't familiar with goings-on at mental institutions, especially those catering for adolescents. The youngest of us was thirteen; the oldest two were eighteen, almost nineteen. They could have been re-assigned to an adult ward but someone had decided that they fitted better, would thrive better, with the rest of our group. I was just sixteen, the fourth youngest. When we were full there were sixteen residents, eight boys and eight girls but the numbers sometimes dropped to 14 or 15 with passes out, abscondings and various crises.

Pills were dispensed from the nurses' station, which also acted as a kind of observation tower between the boys' ward and the girls' ward. Most of the medication we were prescribed would not be prescribed today. Our unit was separate and modern, but was adjacent to the main hospital. We ate meals in an older room, part of the main hospital, with high ceilings and cast iron radiators. We were served by long-term inmates of the adult wards. One elderly man had to be addressed as 'Your Majesty'. As long as you did that, and avoided eye contact with him, there were no problems and no dramas.

One of the nurses was short, Spanish and male. He looked like a frog and his eyes seemed to follow us everywhere. By us, I mean the girls. I never saw him doing anything nurse-like except occasionally dispensing pills. He was obviously quite strong though, as I did see him break up a couple of fights.

Most mornings, we had the option to walk out into the grounds to a small school building. It was like a playhouse and dated from the end of the nineteenth century or the first few years of the twentieth. There were materials for painting and drawing, or we could write or read. There was an eclectic selection of books to borrow. There may have been a piano. There were no actual lessons.

About half of our group never set foot in the school, but I must have spent about half of my mornings there, whenever I was well enough. It was an opportunity to escape the confines of the unit, where it was often hot and airless, where tempers frequently flared up and where hormones raged.

The only teacher at this little schoolhouse was a local woman called Judith. She smiled and was patient. Her voice was low and measured. She had a deep Christian faith and a belief in all of us. Every couple of weeks she took a group of us swimming, a special session just for us. I don't remember if the pool was in the grounds or somewhere else, as she would have needed at least one other staff member had the pool been in the world outside. We used to laugh unkindly at her hairy legs and her very pear-shaped figure. Did she hear our jibes? If she did, nothing was ever said.

Through Judith, I discovered three Elizabeth poets - Elizabeth Barrett Browning, Elizabeth Bishop and Elizabeth Jennings. I was already reading a lot of Dylan Thomas and the Liverpool poets. Poetry was becoming my favourite medium.

The oldest resident in our unit would discharge himself regularly, go off and busk, get into some kind of trouble with drugs, the police or people generally and then check himself back in again. He was tall and skinny, with a full beard and long straight fair hair. He played the guitar beautifully but didn't talk much.

The next girl to me in age was about a year older. She was Eastern European with a troubled background, a series of foster parents and a knack for getting into scrapes, of a sexual nature, every time she was given a pass to go out for the afternoon. She was very attractive, in a curvy, careless, scruffy kind of way. The misadventures she had confirmed her belief that this was her destiny, that she was designed for mistreatment and abuse. She read the tarot cards every morning too.

Some of us were from privileged backgrounds; some were not. We spanned the social spectrum. Some had two parents, some had one and a couple of us were orphans, dependent upon the state and the kindness of strangers. We were of all levels of intellect and aspirations. Sometimes there was violence, against each other or against self. Mostly though, we were bewildered, lost and unhappy.

Froggy would a-wooing go. Froggy? Well he was mostly to be found of an afternoon or an evening, before his shift, during his shift and afterwards too, rifling through drawers and diaries, crawling through the long grass, hoping to catch his teenage charges 'up to something' – indulging in drugs or alcohol, banned stimulants, semi-nude sunbathing, (one of us was partial to this), but desperately hoping to catch a pair of his charges in flagrante delicto and interrupt some coitus. Serious hanky-panky anyway. He was nearly always disappointed but he was a man on a mission, obsessive and voyeuristic, and should never have been allowed anywhere near any of us.

A month or so into my stay there was a new addition – a petite young Australian psychologist, well-dressed, elaborately made up and manicured, an exotic bloom with a sharp wit and a powerful voice which belied her stature. As with the unglamorous Judith, she also took me under her wing and fought my corner when my former headmistress blocked my leaving *her* school – I don't know why - and joining another more relaxed co-educational establishment. This psychologist had an oddly flirtatious relationship with 'Froggy', who couldn't believe his luck. But she was playing him. I don't know what she would have made of the academic psychologist I mention next. Doubtless would have put him firmly in his place too.

He was a youngish psychology academic who had rooms in the grounds of the hospital. A posh, clever man who was later to become famous, notorious even, for some of the political causes he espoused and became passionate about. Back then he was conducting research into the libidos of teenagers - (his research paper probably wasn't called that though). He cherrypicked us. The ones he spoke to, at great length, were two of the more intelligent boys, (aged 15 and 16), and six of the girls (aged 16 and 17), except the two eldest (who were the least academic, the plainest and the most 'down-to-earth') of us. He wanted from us the full details about our sexual experiences, about petting, about masturbation and about our fantasies. No one ever suggested we might need a chaperone when we spoke to him. In all probability, no one knew what he was talking t.

The man in charge of the unit – an eminent psychiatrist – committed suicide sometime after I left.

We were there for our protection but there was a lot that was suspect, highly fishy, going on…I think we all got through it. I hope so. I never saw the boy I was close to after we left hospital. *What happens in the psychiatric unit stays in the psychiatric unit…*

I did stay in contact with Judith, the teacher, for a year or so afterwards. She was disappointed that evangelical Christianity didn't appeal to me. We drifted apart after that.

Ferrets

Have you heard the one about the Argentinian polo player? Of course you have. If it wasn't in the papers, then it must have come from our delightfully outrageous tenant.

We let the converted outbuildings on the side of the house to a small entertainment business. They were ladies who were paid to organise, arrange and style dos, bashes, parties, shindigs and shenanigans for corporate clients, sports events and well-heeled private customers. They were bubbly and funny. They enjoyed first class champagne and very good times. Amongst their clientele were polo clubs and polo players. Which brings me back. Size, of course, isn't everything.

I've used that expression many times as a woman the wrong side of five feet two. Diamonds come in small packages. That one too. My mum was a powerful, strong, short woman. My mother-in-law – diminutive but fierce. So why is it that some women are obsessed with size? In their men. We've all met the cocksure ones, generously endowed with all except intelligence and subtlety.

*

There was a boy known as *the ferret*. His face wasn't at all ferrety. He was dark-haired, dark-eyed, pale skinned and rather beautiful until he smiled or moved. Like a vampire or a rather vicious rodent, he had sharp, pointed teeth. His canines were terrifying. He carried a knife. And he walked with a cocky swagger – a God's gift to women kind of knowing swagger.

I don't know how or why he was on the periphery of the circles I was moving in. He didn't go to one of the local schools. He was older than me, maybe 18 or 19. He wasn't the older brother of anyone I knew. But he appeared from time to time, circling, watching, and in my case, just once when I was off-guard, pouncing too.

*

In my first year as an undergraduate, I became the almost seamless replacement of my second boyfriend's exotic girlfriend. If that makes any sense at all! She was middle European, the blonde, beautiful, brilliant, bohemian and musical daughter of an architect. The family had fled, a couple of years before, to the UK. Her father was Jewish, clever and charismatic. Like me, she adored her father and undermined and undervalued her mother. Unlike me, she didn't seem to have discovered that her father, her hero, was deeply flawed. She played the violin, smoked roll-ups, didn't shave her legs and was on the same course as the second uni boyfriend. Maths with logic. On paper, they had much more in common than he and I did.

What I discovered though was that she had been assaulted, a serious assault just months before she had arrived at uni. Her relationship with my second boyfriend was not consummated. She escaped.

*

There is a condition called *vaginismus*. It's when the muscles of your vagina contract, freeze. Sometimes in reaction to trauma, to assault, sometimes in memory of that assault. This girl – my friend - suffered from it when she embarked on a relationship with her next boyfriend. He was a post-grad, long-legged, slightly pointy of face – an amiable, weirdly-attractive-slightly-ferrety wannabe lover. The panic button was activated, without her having any control over it. Now this man was a kind, considerate and uber-intelligent guy. She sought counselling. I hope they're still together.

I've had *it*, experienced it, three times. On each occasion it protected me from something which shouldn't happen. Didn't happen. Was wrong for me. The first time was on the Isle of Wight. When the boy, who called himself my protector, my pseudo older brother, was foiled by my body's reaction. He wasn't violent, but he

83

was angry. He ran away, smoked things, ignored me. I was three weeks out of hospital, confused and terrified.

It was musically and culturally, a momentous time. Hendrix played. I went back to our tent, was robbed, and stumbled across *the ferret* . Or maybe he stumbled across me. He had been circling. He pounced. I was given a choice and it was no choice at all. I knew by now I was so traumatised that, even if I decided it was the safest option, I wouldn't be able to submit. So I took the other option.

When I made my way back to the port, I had not a penny. My purse had been stolen. I was still virgo-more or less-intacta but I had been forced. By the ferret. To perform fellatio. I suppose you could call it a different sort of rape.

*

Towards the end of my second year at uni, I was in a seminar group looking at seventeenth century poets. One of my fellow students was a mature student, 28 or 29 to our 19 or 20. She was a single mother with a three year old child. She pointed out that, in a couple of poems we were studying, the poet was not seducing his lady. He was coercing her. Bullying her. This wasn't love. It was abuse. The discussion widened.

The mature student had been raped. She had gone to the police. Because she was a single mother, she had been treated badly. The perpetrator had got away.

*

My multiple experiences of sexual harassment and assault were mostly what I would describe as *mild*, almost inconsequential. Rites of passage. But not all. For most of these incidents it would not have occurred to me to go to the police. On the couple of occasions when I did, it was after I was married, after I became a mother, and only when I could not in any sense have been considered to have been putting myself at risk, doing something stupid or provocative or thoughtless. Instinctively, I knew what game I had to play.

On one occasion, at uni, I'd travelled by train one evening from

Brighton to the nearest town to boyfriend number two's family home. There was no-one to meet me. No taxi turned up either. I hitched a lift and, as soon as I was in the car, I knew this had been a bad idea. There were three blokes, all high on something. They took a detour into the woods. I was the next part of their evening's entertainment – an unexpected bonus. I climbed out of the car, cutting my wrist badly on my exit. I ran. And ran. And got away, cut, scratched, scraped, muddy. That was not one I reported.

*

Many years later, on an idyllic summer afternoon, I took a public footpath through the grounds of a prep school. I was with my three young children, a friend and her two children. I was grabbed from behind, groped, fondled and goosed. We went to the headmaster's office and the police were called. I don't think the man was found. Our concern, mine and my friend's, was more for the children at the school.

The other time I did go to the police had been in Bristol. I was twenty-five, in my first trimester of pregnancy for baby number two. A man followed me from all the way from Broadmead in the centre of Bristol. I was pushing a buggy. There's a gradual and horrible realisation when you know you're being followed, you can't see anyone around who could help you, and you're pregnant, you're on a steep hill, and you can't let go of the buggy as the brake might not hold. You use what you have. The buggy becomes a battering ram hitting his thighs and his groin; you run over his feet repeatedly till he yelps in pain. You find your scream.

The policewoman shocked me. She suggested that I should have been flattered. After all, I was married, pregnant, wearing a loose, summery dress. *Wasn't it actually great to be fancied?* I only had to deal with her once.

The male police officer I had contact from then on was much more sympathetic. He let me know that the man who followed me, who assaulted me but was thwarted in his intentions, was wanted for many alleged offences of indecent assault, assault, attempted rape and rape. He pleaded guilty and then, just before the case came to trial, he

85

changed his plea. I was going to have to give evidence in court. It was just a week or two from my due date. I didn't sleep. This wasn't what I had been expecting. On the morning I was due to give evidence, he changed his plea to guilty again. He was convicted. I had my second child two and a half weeks later.

*

Much, much earlier, when I was fifteen, my mother berated the staff at the Dairy just behind the milk bar and coffee shop I was working in alone. My colleague was on the fortnight's holiday she'd unsuccessfully tried to lose weight for.

I had banged on the wall and shouted. No one came to my aid. The middle-aged, middle European loner had locked me in the shop, robbed the till, fondled and stroked me, told me he was taking me away with him. He had a knife. I don't think he'd have used it, but he wouldn't have needed to. I was five and a half stones. He was about seventeen stones. Maybe a little more. I emerged unscathed having discovered strength, wit and cunning in my moment of need. I told my mother everything. She was sad, angry and outraged. She expected my employers to step up. The police weren't called. Everything was ok. That was my last job before the breakdown.

*

The second uni boyfriend's family was complicated. They had a big house, a kind of stately home. Bigger than a manor house, not as big as Blenheim. His mother was American. His father was Hungarian, a baronet. There was a woman and her child who lived in a cottage in the grounds. I was told she was a mistress, or former mistress, of the father. There was a man who lived somewhere, either in the grounds, or close by. He was a maintenance man, or handyman, or groundsperson. I forget which. Maybe it was all of them. Apparently, he bred ferrets and was in love with my boyfriend's mother.

She looked remarkably like a slightly less appealing Anjelica Huston in The Addams Family, or Yvonne de Carlo. I'd watched her, (Yvonne de Carlo), with my father on the very first black and white TV our family owned – the one *he* made for my bedroom when I was

86

a sickly six-year-old.

This real, flesh-and-blood woman, the scary mother of a boy I was involved with, loved the boa constrictor in his/her tank in their vast kitchen. I'm not a snake afficionado but know rodents, usually dead, are a delicacy. The woman fed live animals to her snake. I saw her do it. They were an unusual family and they didn't like me.

*

As an animal lover, I've witnessed cruelty. As a woman, I'm proud to have muddled through a lot of mess. Yes, it was complicated. Yes, you picked your fights. The ones you knew you might, could, win. Everything else was chalked up to experience. I don't know how *normal* it's all been. I suppose it doesn't matter much in the grand scheme of things – if there is one.

And I really am still so optimistic, so positive about life, about men and about the human race.

Ingram Content Group UK Ltd.
Milton Keynes UK
UKHW031419270423
420877UK00016B/943